Grandmother's Recipes

Grandmother's Recipes

TRADITIONAL FOOD FROM THE HEART OF THE HOME

JANE MAPLE

ARCTURUS

This book is intended as an informal guide to life, health and household. While every effort has been made to ensure this book contains warnings, where necessary, about the possible dangers of substances mentioned herein, it may be advisable to consult a qualified medical practitioner before use. The publisher, the editor and their respective employees shall not accept responsibility for injury, loss or damage occasioned to any person acting or refraining from action as a result of material in this book, whether or not such injury, loss or damage is in any way due to negligent act or omission on the part of the publisher, editor or employees.

ARCTURUS

This edition published in 2011 by Arcturus Publishing Limited
26/27 Bickels Yard, 151–153 Bermondsey Street,
London SE1 3HA

ISBN: 978-1-84858-077-0
AD001907EN

Printed in China

Contents

Introduction

Picture if you can an old kitchen with a flagstone floor, a solid fuel range cooker standing along one wall and a few pots and pans hanging from old meat hooks by the one and only work surface. A large white butler sink is positioned beneath the kitchen window which overlooks the garden, and a table and chairs stand in the corner where everyone gathers on a regular basis. This describes the kitchen where I was raised, deep in the countryside. In grandmother's day it was quite normal for the entire family to gravitate towards the kitchen – not only did it smell wonderful but it was warm and cosy long before the days of central heating. I can see it now, a great big pan of porridge gently bubbling on top of the stove and next to it an equally large pan filled with a wonderful-smelling soup for grandfather's lunch after a morning of working in the fields. Add to these smells the aroma of fresh bread and I know there is no place I would rather be.

I would like to take you on a culinary adventure to uncover some of grandmother's passions. Today, food has become subject to the vagaries of fashion, and somewhere along the way the traditional methods of cooking have been lost. Grandmother did not have numerous colourful cookbooks to follow and fancy presentation was not an issue – she just used what she had in the larder and made the best food she could. Her recipes were in her head, most probably handed down from generation to generation, and if she wanted to know if something tasted as it should she simply dipped her finger in and judged by experience. Grandmother worked with ingredients that were available at that time of year and within her meagre budget, but her family never went hungry. She took her time in a steady, relaxed manner, whether she was kneading bread dough or rolling out puff pastry. Stress was not something she experienced – not in the kitchen, anyway.

Grandmother did not have an array of fancy gadgets to make her life easier – they simply were not available and even if they had been she would not have been able to afford them. I remember to this day the old clay pot which stood on the worktop, with its assorted array of wooden spoons, a metal whisk that was starting to become distorted from overuse and an old steel used for sharpening her two kitchen knives. She also had an old wooden rolling pin, a metal flour shaker and a small spiky contraption which she used to tenderize her meat. She had one wooden chopping board which sufficed for everything and all tasks were done by hand.

Grandmother's kitchen did not have the luxury of a fridge, just a cool cabinet that had a mesh front to keep the flies out. There were no kitchen cupboards, just a giant walk-in larder by which, as a child, I was fascinated. The shelves were stocked with jars of pickles and jams, all labelled with the date and contents, large pots that stored items such as flour, porridge oats, dried beans and sugar, and a blue and white spotted dish that always contained a pat of rich yellow butter. Also around the kitchen were various herbs carefully tied in small bunches with string and then hung up to dry. Kept in the shed at the bottom of the garden were sacks of potatoes, turnips and swedes, and always a few boxes of cooking apples carefully kept apart by rolled-up newspaper. That was grandfather's department – he worked the garden and allotment and kept the kitchen supplied with vegetables throughout the year. The garden itself had rows of fruit bushes – blackcurrants, redcurrants, gooseberries, raspberries, loganberries and strawberry plants – that he had carefully grown in hanging boxes to save his back from too much bending over.

I hope that you will try some of these traditional recipes and that, once you grow in culinary confidence, you will start to put your own personal touches to them – never be afraid to experiment, as that is the secret of a good cook. I also hope that you enjoy this book as much as I have enjoyed writing it and that you will find the delight of grandmother's secrets that are in its pages.

Grandmother grabbed the rolling pin
And rolled the pastry out, nice and thin
To cover the apples spiced with cloves
To put in the oven with the two round loaves

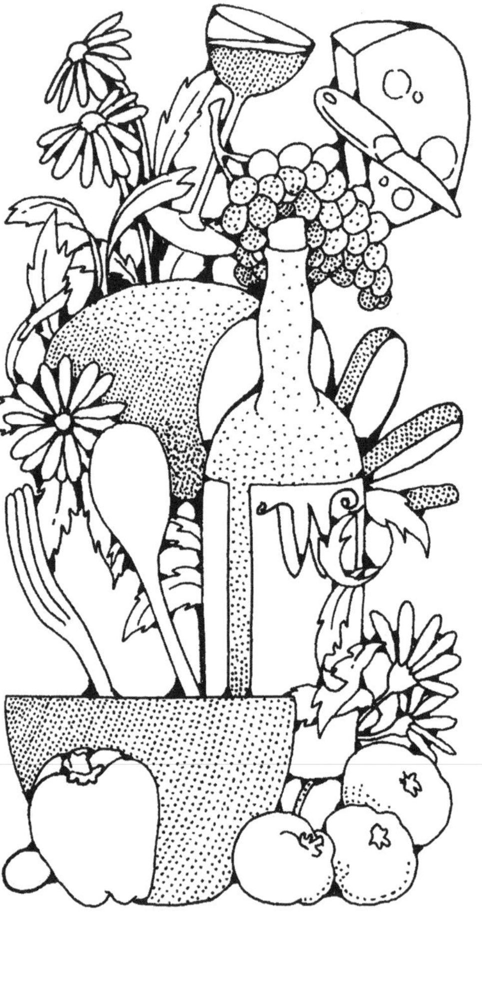

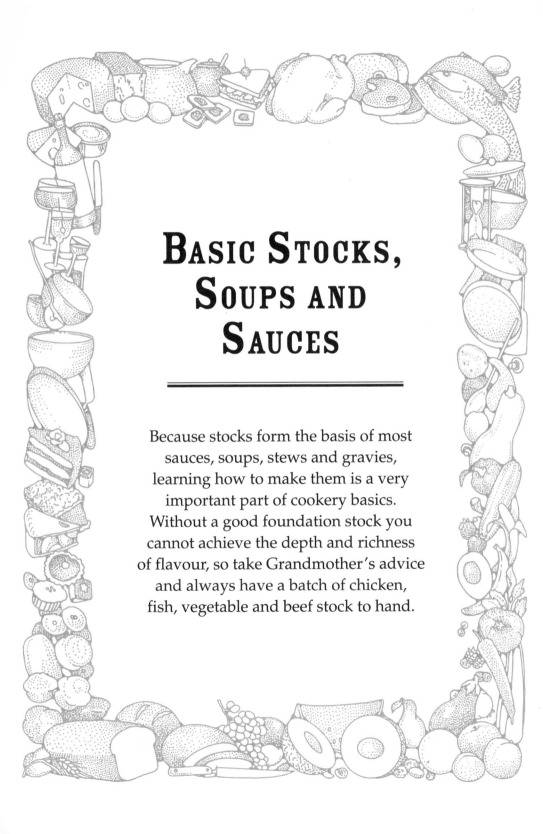

Basic Stocks, Soups and Sauces

Because stocks form the basis of most sauces, soups, stews and gravies, learning how to make them is a very important part of cookery basics. Without a good foundation stock you cannot achieve the depth and richness of flavour, so take Grandmother's advice and always have a batch of chicken, fish, vegetable and beef stock to hand.

Basic Stocks

The basis of many recipes is a good-quality stock, created from scratch rather than from a shop-bought cube. Stock is a liquid reduction made from vegetables, fish or meat which, with the correct amount of cooking and seasoning, possesses a rich, intense flavour. A good stock does take time and effort, but it is worth while as it will give that extra-special flavour to your finished dish. While you are at it, make a reasonable quantity as you can store the stock in individual portions in airtight containers in your freezer for later use. One of the easiest ways of storing it is to make your own cubes by pouring the finished liquid into ice-cube trays; once they are frozen, you can put these cubes into airtight containers and use them as necessary.

The other great thing about stock is that it is made from the parts of the meat, fish, or vegetables that would otherwise be discarded, using up every bit of food available. We live in a throw-away age, but as we are becoming more and more aware of recycling and the amount of food we tend to waste, we are realizing that using as much of it as possible makes sense not only to our environment but to our purses as well.

BONES

When making a meat stock, bones are a vital ingredient, particularly knuckle bones as these contain collagen which, when simmered, forms gelatine to help the stock set. One point to remember, though, is that the stock must be cooled to 21°C (70°F) within one hour to prevent bacteria forming.

USING COLD WATER

It is vital to start a stockpot using cold water, as a protein called albumen will only dissolve in cold water. The release of albumen results in a much clearer stock as it rises to the surface as scum, bearing with it any impurities.

THE BASIC INGREDIENTS

When making any kind of stock you will need four basic ingredients that will give a rich, earthy flavour to the finished recipe. These are:

Bouquet garni
Carrots
Celery
Onions

What is a bouquet garni?

You can buy bouquets garnis, but it is very easy to make your own. A bouquet garni is simply a collection of fresh herbs – traditionally parsley, thyme, bay leaves and sage – tied together in a bundle or enclosed in a small muslin bag so that they can easily be removed at the end of cooking. This gives the recipe a subtle flavour without the herbs overpowering the other ingredients.

Chicken Stock

Makes approximately 600 ml (1 pint)

1 chicken carcass and any leftover chicken
2 carrots, roughly chopped
2 celery sticks, roughly chopped
2 onions, peeled and quartered
4 garlic cloves, whole
1 bouquet garni
salt and freshly ground black pepper to taste

Method

- Put the chicken carcass into a large saucepan, then add the carrots, celery, onion, garlic cloves and bouquet garni. Pour in approximately 1 litre (1¾ pints) cold water or enough to make sure that the carcass and vegetables are totally immersed. Add a little salt and pepper and then bring to the boil. Lower the heat and simmer for 2–3 hours without a lid.
- Take off the heat and allow to cool, after first removing any scum that may have settled on the surface with a slotted spoon.
- Once the liquid has cooled enough to handle, strain through a sieve into a clean saucepan. Carefully remove the bones, meat and bouquet garni from the sieve and then, using the back of a spoon, squash the vegetables through the sieve as this will give your finished stock a wonderful sweet taste.
- Now, to make the flavour more intense, put the stock back on the heat and boil gently until it has reduced by half the volume. Taste and season to your liking.
- Allow the stock to cool completely, then pour into ice-cube trays and place in the freezer. Once they are frozen you can pop the individual cubes out of the tray, place them in a freezer bag or plastic container and return to the freezer until you are ready to use them.

Beef Stock

Although this stock takes a long time to cook, it is really worth making the effort as it is a wonderful base for so many meat dishes and gravies. The meat bones give it an incredible depth of flavour, far superior than any shop-bought stock cube.

Makes approximately 600 ml (1 pint)

2 carrots, sliced in half lengthways
2 onions, quartered, with the skin still on
2 celery sticks or celery tops, whole

2 garlic cloves, whole
2 kg (4½ lb) beef bones
2 tbsp vegetable oil
salt and freshly ground black pepper to taste
1 bouquet garni

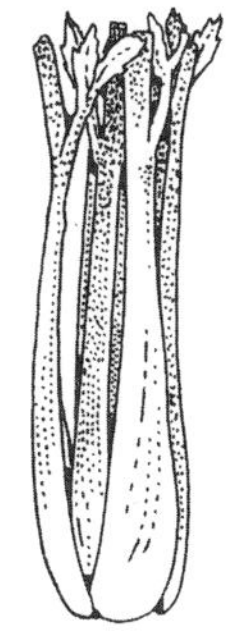

Method

- Preheat the oven to 200°C (400°F/Gas mark 6).
- Place all the vegetables and the garlic in the bottom of a large roasting tin.
- Place the bones on top of the vegetables, pour the vegetable oil over and season with salt and pepper. Roast in the oven for 1 hour.
- Remove the bones and vegetables from the oven and place them in a large saucepan. Pour in enough cold water to make sure the bones and vegetables are immersed and add the bouquet garni. Bring to the boil and then turn the heat down to low. Remove any foam that is floating on the surface using a slotted spoon.
- Simmer the stock for about 6 hours, periodically removing any fatty scum that floats to the surface.
- At the end of the cooking time, remove the stock from the heat and allow to cool until it is safe to handle. Using a fine sieve, strain the liquid into another large saucepan. Remove all the bones and the bouquet garni and then, using the back of a spoon, press the vegetables through the sieve to add flavour.
- Return the saucepan to a medium heat and simmer the stock again until the volume is reduced by half, skimming off any scum that appears on the surface.

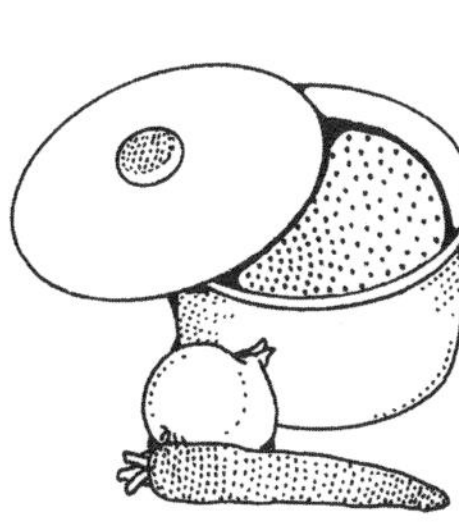

- Allow the stock to cool completely then pour into ice-cube trays and place them in the freezer. Once the stock cubes are completely frozen you can pop them out of the ice-cube tray and store as suggested on page 10.

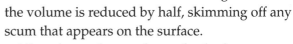

Vegetable Stock

This vegetable stock does not take as long to cook as the beef stock and is a useful base for many soups and sauces. It also uses up parts of the vegetables that would otherwise be wasted, such as the peel and the tops. You can use any vegetables you like to make this stock, in addition, of course, to the basic ingredients mentioned on page 11. Although you should not use any vegetables that are starting to go mouldy, it does not matter if they are starting to wilt a little – you will not sacrifice any flavour if your ingredients are a few days old. Mushrooms work well if you want a slightly 'earthy' flavour, while if you want a sweeter end result, add a few sweetcorn kernels. Be careful if you are adding cabbage, though – it is best to use only the sweeter, inner leaves as the dark green ones can give a rather bitter taste to the stock. I have not given exact measurements for the ingredients in this stock; just add enough of the vegetables listed below to half fill a large saucepan. Approximately 900 g (2 lb) should be sufficient.

Makes approximately 600 ml (1 pint)

carrot, parsnip and leek, roughly chopped, including peelings and tops
2 celery sticks, roughly chopped
cauliflower, broccoli and asparagus stalks, roughly chopped
2 large onions, quartered
6–8 peppercorns
1 tsp salt (or to taste)
1 bouquet garni
1 garlic clove, whole

Method

- Place all the ingredients in a large saucepan or stockpot.
- Add enough cold water to cover the vegetables totally and then bring to the boil.
- Reduce the heat and simmer the stock for about 30–40 minutes, periodically skimming off any scum that has formed on the surface using

a slotted spoon. Remove from the heat and allow to cool so that it is safe to handle.

- Drain the stock through a fine sieve into a clean saucepan, pressing the cooked vegetables through the sieve using the back of a spoon.
- Return the stock to the heat and simmer until the volume has reduced by half to make the flavour more intense.
- Allow to cool completely and freeze in ice-cube trays (see page 10).

Fish Stock

Like the vegetable stock, this stock uses up odds and ends that you would otherwise throw away, such as the heads, bones and tails. You can also add the trimmings from prawns, as this will make the final flavour even richer. This does not keep as well as the other stocks so if you do not intend to freeze it, make sure you use it the same day. It is well worth experimenting with this stock by adding either some lemon juice or a glass of dry white wine during the final stage of cooking.

Makes approximately 600 ml (1 pint)

900 g (2 lb) trimmings from fish such as cod, haddock, plaice, sea bream, turbot or brill
2 tbsp vegetable oil
1 leek, roughly sliced
2 celery sticks, chopped
2 carrots, roughly chopped
1 fennel bulb, roughly chopped
1 large onion, roughly chopped
2 garlic cloves, halved
1 bouquet garni
salt and white pepper to taste

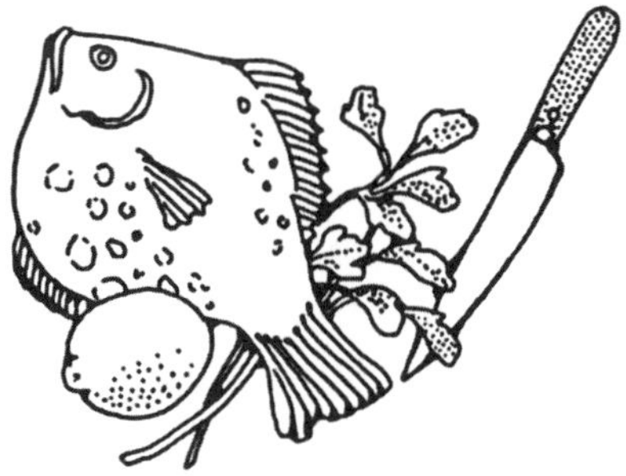

Method

- Wash all the fish trimmings in cold water, making sure you remove the eyes and any bloody innards as these can make the final stock cloudy and a little bitter. Put the trimmings in a large saucepan or stockpot and add enough cold water to cover them.
- Heat the vegetable oil in another pan and add all the vegetables and garlic. Fry gently until they start to soften, but do not allow them to go brown.
- Add the cooked vegetables to the pan containing the fish trimmings, then add the bouquet garni and seasoning. Bring the stock to the boil, then turn down the heat and simmer for about 30 minutes, periodically removing the scum from the surface using a slotted spoon.
- Remove the stock from the heat and allow it to cool so that it is safe to handle. Strain the stock into a clean pan through a piece of muslin to make sure that no fine bones are left in the final liquid.
- This stock does not need reducing as further cooking will only ruin the flavour. Cool it and use on the same day or freeze in ice-cube trays (see page 10).

Grandmother's Tips for Making Fish Stock

- Ask your fishmonger for any unwanted fish carcasses – they usually have plenty that are just thrown away after they have filleted a fish for a customer.
- For a truly luxurious fish stock, use raw shells from crab, crayfish, lobster, clams and mussels.
- While meat stocks improve with cooking, 45 minutes is the maximum time that a fish stock should be cooked for, as it starts to lose its rich flavour after this time.
- To make a nice spicy alternative, add 1 teaspoon of smoked paprika at the end of the cooking time.

Soups

Soups can be thick and chunky, smooth and creamy or clear and spicy – there is no set rule. They can include anything you want and they are a great way of making a nutritious meal all in one pot. Nothing fills you up and comforts you on a chilly day the same way that a bowl of homemade soup does. You can use up leftovers and combine them with some fresh ingredients to make a variety of wonderfully tasty meals. Before giving you some of my favourite recipes, I want to let you in on some of my tips for making successful and easy soups:

- Make a soup a day in advance, as this allows the flavours to infuse.
- Do not add much salt to the soup until you have finished the reducing period, which makes all the flavours much stronger. Add more seasoning at the end until you get it just right.
- If you do find that a soup is too salty, you can rectify that by adding half a peeled raw potato to absorb the excess salt. Simmer for about 15 minutes and then remove the potato.
- If you are making a tomato soup you might find it a little too acidic for your liking. To adjust this simply add a teaspoon of sugar to make it more palatable.
- You do not need to add thickeners to soup. If you want a more sturdy broth, whizz some of the vegetables in a blender with a little of the liquid and return to the soup.
- Instead of using plain water, reserve some vegetable cooking water as this will improve the flavour of your soup.
- Except for the bouquet garni, add fresh herbs towards the end of cooking to preserve their full flavour.

Pea and Mint Soup

Here is my recipe for a wonderful soup which is not only really healthy but also delicious and can be served either hot or cold. This recipe can be made with either frozen or freshly shelled garden peas; both work extremely well so it is not limited to the period when this versatile vegetable is in season. It is wonderfully creamy and will always remind me of the freshness of spring with its vibrant green colouring.

Serves 4

25 g (1 oz) butter
1 large onion, finely chopped
3 celery sticks, finely chopped
1 large potato, cut into small chunks
1 kg (2¼ lb) fresh or frozen peas
200 ml (7 fl oz) chicken or vegetable stock (see pages 11–12 and 14–15)
salt and freshly ground black pepper
10 mint leaves, plus 8 to garnish
1 tbsp double cream

Method

- Melt the butter in a large frying pan. Add the onion and celery to the pan and sauté gently until they are soft and just starting to turn brown.
- Meanwhile, place the potato in a large saucepan and then add the peas, chicken or vegetable stock and a small pinch of salt. Add the cooked onion and celery and then bring to the boil. Turn down the heat and simmer for about 20 minutes.
- Remove the soup from the heat and allow it to cool down a little before placing it in a blender with the mint leaves. Blend until the soup has a creamy consistency.
- Taste the soup and season it to your liking. Transfer to 4 bowls. Just before serving, swirl some double cream into the surface and add a couple of mint leaves for extra garnish.

Grandmother's Tips

- If you would prefer to have the soup with some of the peas left whole, remove some from the stock with a slotted spoon before putting the liquid into the blender.

- For a special treat, fry tiny pieces of streaky bacon until they are brown and crispy and float them on the surface of the soup before serving.

Freezing Peas

Peas are one of the vegetables that taste nearly as good frozen as they do freshly picked from the garden. If you have enough space make sure you grow enough in your garden or allotment so that you have plenty to see you through the winter. Because peas contain a lot of sugar it is essential to blanch them before freezing so that they retain their colour and sweet flavour. This is very simple if you follow these steps:

- Shell the peas and wash them in cold water.

- Fill a large saucepan half full with water and bring to the boil.

- Pour in the peas and allow them to cook for 2–3 minutes.

- While the peas are cooking, fill a large bowl with cold water and add a few ice cubes.

- Drain the peas and drop them immediately into the ice-cold water.

- Divide the peas into family-sized portions and put into freezer bags. Make sure you always label the bags with the date and use up within 6 months.

Leek and Potato Soup

This was one of my favourite winter warmers when I was a child; Grandmother always had a supply of potatoes and onions in store and Grandfather pulled leeks out of the allotment when required. This type of soup has stood the test of time and is very often found on the menu boards of country pubs, probably because it is as popular today as it was when I was a child. If you want to be posh you can call it Vichyssoise. The true Vichyssoise, however, was served cold and originated in New York City at the beginning of the 20th century, created by a chef who worked at the fashionable Ritz-Carlton Hotel on Madison Avenue.

Serves 4

25 g (1 oz) butter
4 large leeks, sliced
1 large onion, roughly chopped
175 g (6 oz) potatoes, cut into small cubes
salt and freshly ground black pepper
900 ml (1½ pints) vegetable stock (see pages 14–15)
2 tbsp double cream
fresh chives, snipped

Method

- Melt the knob of butter in a heavy-based saucepan. Add the leeks, onion and potatoes, stirring them with a wooden spoon to make sure they are completely covered in the butter. Season with a little salt and pepper, place the lid on the saucepan and turn the heat down to low. Using a lid will help to create steam inside the saucepan which allows the vegetables to sweat rather than fry, giving them a nice rich flavour.
- Next, add the vegetable stock and bring to a gentle simmer. Replace the lid and allow the soup to cook gently for a further 20 minutes or until the vegetables are completely soft.

- Remove the soup from the heat and allow it to cool slightly before whizzing it in a blender. You may need to do this in batches, so make sure you have another pan ready to put the first batch into.
- When you are ready to serve, reheat the soup gently, pour into 4 bowls and swirl some double cream on top. Sprinkle the chives over and serve.

Grandmother's Cheesy Croûtons

Leek and potato soup tastes even better when served with some cheesy croûtons. They take no time at all to make and are great for using up bread that has gone a little stale. Cut the bread into slices and toast under the grill until lightly browned. Top with some grated Gruyère cheese and pop back under the grill until the cheese is bubbling and starting to brown. Cut the slices into tiny squares and float them on top of the soup just before serving – scrummy!

Chicken Soup with Noodles

There is nothing that will warm you up quicker than a steaming bowl of chicken soup when the weather is bitterly cold. Did you know, however, that it is also very beneficial if you are suffering from a cold? If anyone in my family is feeling a little under the weather I always make them a nice mug of chicken soup to sip, but for a hearty lunch add some noodles to make it go even further.

Serves 4

1 medium-sized chicken (about 1.8 kg/4 lb in weight)
salt and freshly ground black pepper
2 large onions, roughly chopped
2 large carrots, roughly chopped
3 celery sticks, roughly chopped
2 garlic cloves, left whole
6 whole black peppercorns
4 fresh parsley sprigs, plus extra for garnish
225 g (8 oz) egg noodles

Method

- Place the chicken whole in a large saucepan. Half fill the pan with cold water and add a little salt.
- Bring to the boil and then reduce the heat to low so that the liquid simmers gently. From time to time, skim the foam from the surface using a slotted spoon.
- After 40 minutes, add the onions, carrots, celery, garlic, peppercorns and parsley and bring back to the boil. Lower the heat once more and allow the soup to simmer gently for 1 hour. It is very important that you do not cook the soup too quickly at this stage otherwise the end result will be cloudy.
- When the hour is up, pierce the chicken with a knife to check if the juices run clear. If the chicken is not cooked through, leave it to simmer for a little longer and check the juices again.

- When you are certain the chicken is thoroughly cooked, remove it from the cooking juices and allow it to cool so that you can handle it comfortably. Discard the skin and remove the flesh from the bones, putting it by to use in another recipe. Return the bones to the pan and simmer for another 2–2½ hours.
- Strain the liquid through a large sieve lined with a piece of muslin and discard the bones and vegetables.
- Chill the soup in the fridge to allow the fat to settle on the surface. Remove the fat and transfer the soup to a clean saucepan. Add the noodles and some thin strips of the cooked chicken breast and allow the soup to cook for 7 minutes or until the noodles are tender.
- Season the soup to taste before serving and sprinkle with some freshly chopped parsley.

Grandmother's Best Cold and Flu Remedy

As a child I always believed what Grandmother said was true, but as an adult I have started to doubt some of her tales. However, in the case of chicken soup being a remedy for colds and flu, interestingly enough scientific evidence supports her theory. Apparently, traditionally made chicken soup does have certain healing properties. Items such as garlic and pepper that are added to the soup work in a similar way to cough medicine by helping to thin mucus and therefore making breathing easier. Amino acids released from the chicken during cooking resemble a drug that is prescribed for bronchitis and the hot, steamy liquid helps to flush away those nasty viruses that leave us feeling under the weather.

Oxtail Soup

Originally, oxtail really did come from the tail of an ox – this was in the days when every part of an animal was used for some recipe or other. Today, however, it is the tail of a beef cow. Although it is not as easy to find as it was in former times, ask your butcher if he has some or if he can order some in for you. Slow cooking brings out the full flavour of the oxtail and makes a wonderful soup, so do not be put off by the lengthy cooking process.

Serves 6

1 tbsp plain flour, seasoned with salt and pepper
1 large oxtail, trimmed of fat and cut into small pieces
75 g (2½ oz) unsalted butter
1 tbsp vegetable oil
1 onion, whole
3 cloves
8 black peppercorns
1 bouquet garni
3 celery sticks, roughly chopped
1 carrot, sliced
1 turnip, sliced
2.2 litres (4 pints) water
salt and freshly ground black pepper
4 tbsp sherry

Method

- Put the seasoned flour into a large plastic freezer bag and add the oxtail. Seal the bag and shake until the oxtail is completely covered with flour.
- Combine the butter and oil in a large frying pan – using a combination of the two will prevent the butter from burning. Once the butter has melted and the pan is nice and hot add the floured oxtail and brown on all sides.
- Peel the onion, then push the three cloves into the sides.
- Remove the oxtail from the frying pan and place in a large saucepan

together with the peppercorns, bouquet garni, onion, vegetables and water. Season with a little salt and and bring to the boil. Reduce the heat to the lowest possible setting and simmer for at least 2 hours or until the meat is starting to fall off the bone.

- Remove the pan from the heat and allow the soup to cool. Strain through a large sieve lined with muslin. Remove the meat and put it aside in the fridge, then discard the vegetables and bones. Place the soup in a bowl in the fridge and leave overnight.
- In the morning you will find that the soup has turned to a jelly because of the collagen released from the bones during cooking. Remove the layer of fat that has formed on the surface and return the jelly to a clean saucepan along with the reserved meat. Gently heat the soup (do not allow it to boil) and add the sherry just before serving.

Pumpkin Soup

This soup was introduced to my family by my sister, who spent the majority of her life in New England in the United States. As far as soup recipes go, it could not get much easier and the end result is a lovely creamy, sweet soup that goes really well with fresh, crusty bread.

Serves 4

25 g (1 oz) unsalted butter
1 large onion, roughly chopped
2 garlic cloves, crushed
800 g (1¾ lb) pumpkin, peeled and cut into cubes
½ tsp ground cumin
1 tsp sweet paprika
1 litre (1¾ pints) vegetable stock (see pages 14–15)
salt and freshly ground black pepper
2 tbsp double cream
fresh chives, snipped

Method

- Place a large saucepan over a medium heat and add the butter. Allow it to brown but keep an eye on it to make sure it does not burn. Add the onion and garlic and cook until the onion becomes translucent.
- Next, add the pumpkin and stir to combine. Cook gently until the pumpkin starts to soften.
- Add the cumin and paprika and cook for another couple of minutes. Pour in the stock and bring to the boil. Reduce the heat and simmer until the pumpkin is completely soft and starts to break up.
- Remove the soup from the heat and allow to cool, then whizz it in a blender until it is completely smooth. You may need to do this in batches, so make sure you have a clean pan or bowl ready to take the first batch.
- Pour the soup into a clean saucepan and bring it back to a simmer. Continue to cook until the mixture has started to thicken.
- Serve in individual bowls with a swirl of cream on the top and a scattering of chives. Add a crusty roll on the side.

Cream of Artichoke Soup

This soup is made with Jerusalem artichokes, which are a completely different vegetable to globe artichokes. They look similar to root ginger, with their light brown skin and rather knobbly appearance, with crisp, white flesh that resembles the texture of a water chestnut. Look for tubers that are firm, and buy more than you think you need as you tend to lose quite a bit of their flesh when you peel them. Once peeled, they will need to be put swiftly into acidulated water to prevent them from going brown. This recipe makes a beautifully creamy, fragrant soup with a flavour all of its own.

Serves 4

900 g (2 lb) Jerusalem artichokes
2 slices of lemon
salt and freshly ground black pepper

enough milk to make the cooking liquid up to 900 ml (1½ pints)
25 g (1 oz) unsalted butter
1 onion, chopped
1 tbsp cornflour
1–2 tbsp freshly squeezed lemon juice
2 tbsp finely chopped fresh parsley
4 tbsp single cream

Method

- Place the artichokes in a large saucepan with the lemon slices and add enough cold water to cover. Add a little salt and bring to the boil. Reduce the heat and simmer gently for about 20 minutes or until the artichokes are tender.
- Drain the artichokes through a sieve, reserving the liquid in another saucepan. Make up the liquid to 900 ml (1½ pints) with the milk.
- Discard the lemon slices and then mash the artichokes using a potato masher or fork.
- Melt the butter in a clean saucepan, add the onion and cook for about 5 minutes or until translucent – do not allow it to brown otherwise it will discolour the soup. Take the pan off the heat, stir in the cornflour and gradually add the reserved cooking liquid and milk.
- Add the mashed artichokes to the pan and bring to the boil, stirring constantly. Cook for 3–4 minutes, or until the soup has started to thicken.
- Allow the soup to cool and either put it in a blender or rub through a fine sieve using the back of a wooden spoon. Stir in the lemon juice, parsley and fresh cream and season to taste. Heat gently before serving.

Sauces

Sauces are designed to complement a meal and no kitchen cupboard should be without a few of the all-time favourites. However, wouldn't it be nice to make your own sauce knowing that there are no strange ingredients or preservatives in the finished product? Sauces are not difficult to make and can be stored in the fridge quite safely for several weeks, so next time your child or grandchild asks for some ketchup to dip their chips into, offer a bottle of your own.

Tomato Ketchup

Makes approximately 500 ml (16 fl oz)

2 kg (4½ lb) ripe tomatoes, roughly chopped
2 onions, roughly chopped
2 eating apples, peeled and roughly chopped
2 garlic cloves, finely chopped
150 ml (¼ pint) red wine vinegar
100 ml (3½ fl oz) water
½ tsp black peppercorns
½ tsp English mustard powder
1 tsp allspice
1 tsp ground cloves
2 bay leaves
1 tbsp light brown sugar
salt and freshly ground black pepper

Method

- Place the tomatoes, onions, apples and garlic in a large stainless steel saucepan with 50 ml (2 fl oz) vinegar and the water. Bring to the boil, reduce the heat and simmer for 40 minutes, stirring occasionally. Check that the vegetables have reduced to a pulp – if there are still a few solid pieces, cook for a further 10 minutes.

- Pour the remaining vinegar into a clean stainless steel saucepan and add all the spices. Cook over a low heat for 10 minutes to allow the flavours to infuse, then remove from the heat and set aside.
- Rub the tomato mixture through a fine sieve, using the back of a spoon, to remove the tomato skins and seeds.
- Put the tomato purée into a clean saucepan. Strain the infused vinegar through some muslin and add to the pan. Add the sugar and bring to the boil, stirring continuously until the sugar has completely dissolved. Reduce the heat and simmer until the tomato mixture thickens – you should be left with approximately 500 ml (16 fl oz).
- Remove from the heat and season to taste with salt and pepper. Pour into hot, sterilized jars or bottles and seal immediately.

Basic Tomato Sauce

This is another staple sauce that can be used in many recipes, so it is worth making a large batch which can either be stored in jars or in the freezer – frozen in ice-cube trays, it can be easily thawed when you want a small quantity for something quickly made. It is light, very quick to prepare and makes a great accompaniment to pasta.

Serves 4

2 tbsp olive oil
1 onion, finely chopped
1 celery stick, finely chopped
450 g (1 lb) ripe tomatoes, skinned (see page 30) and deseeded
1 tsp sweet paprika
handful of basil leaves, torn
salt and freshly ground black pepper

Method

- Heat the oil in a large frying pan or saucepan and sauté the onion and celery until the onion becomes translucent – do not allow it to brown.
- Cut the tomato flesh into small pieces and add to the pan, together with the paprika and basil.
- Simmer the sauce on a low heat for about 30 minutes or until it starts to thicken. If you find it becomes too dry, add a small amount of water or a little more olive oil.
- Pour the liquid into hot jars and seal immediately. Alternatively, allow the sauce to cool, place in containers and store in the freezer.

Grandmother's Tip for Skinning Tomatoes

Many recipes call for tomatoes to be skinned. To do this easily, place the tomatoes in just-boiled water for 1–1½ minutes and you will see that the skins start to split. Remove the tomatoes from the water and allow to cool. You will then be able to pull the skin away from the flesh with your fingers.

Basic White Sauce

White sauce is used in many recipes, for example to accompany pasta, fish, chicken or cheese dishes. It can be adapted to suit your recipe by adding cheese, herbs, chopped eggs, or indeed anything else you fancy. It really is very easy to make and takes less than 10 minutes, so do not be tempted to cheat and buy a packet mix which will not compare in flavour. If you have tried making white sauce before and found that it was lumpy, there are just two simple tips to follow for a sauce that is smooth and almost silky in appearance: make sure you use cold milk, and allow the flour and butter mixture to cool down a little before you start adding the milk.

Makes approximately 600 ml (1 pint)

50 g (2 oz) unsalted butter
50 g (2 oz) plain flour
½ tsp English mustard powder
600 ml (1 pint) milk
salt and freshly ground black pepper

Method

- Melt the butter over a low heat in a saucepan that has a heavy base to prevent the sauce from burning. Remove the pan from the heat and stir in the flour and mustard powder until they are thoroughly combined and the mixture starts to leave the sides of the pan.
- With the pan still away from the heat, gradually whisk in the milk a little at a time.
- Once you have added all the milk, return the pan to the heat and bring the sauce to the boil, whisking continuously. Reduce the heat and simmer gently for 5 minutes to cook the flour, stirring occasionally to prevent it from sticking.
- Taste and season to your liking. At this stage you can add cheese, chopped parsley, or whatever ingredients your recipe calls for.

Tartare Sauce

This is a thick, piquant sauce that is typically served with fish or seafood. The secret to a good tartare sauce is finding the correct balance between the astringency of the vinegar and the creaminess of the mayonnaise, so it is a good idea to practise until you get it right before serving it to guests. You can use ready-made mayonnaise, but I believe the flavour is much more authentic if you make your own.

Makes approximately 500 ml (16 fl oz)

2 egg yolks
1 tsp Dijon mustard
salt and freshly ground black pepper
250 ml (8 fl oz) olive oil
250 ml (8 fl oz) sunflower oil
juice of ½ lemon
1 tbsp chopped fresh dill
1 tbsp capers
1 tbsp finely chopped gherkins

Method

- Start by making a mayonnaise. Mix the egg yolks with the mustard and a little salt and pepper. Gradually whisk in the two different oils, adding only about a tablespoon at a time. The mixture should be quite thick and creamy at this stage.
- Add the lemon juice, dill, capers and gherkin and stir well to combine. Test the seasoning and adjust as necessary.

Bread Sauce

Bread sauce is one of those old traditional recipes that seems to have fallen out of favour with modern cooks. It is a perfect accompaniment to roast chicken or turkey and is one that you should definitely try as it is sure to go down well with your family.

Serves 6

300 ml (10 fl oz) milk
200 ml (7 fl oz) single cream
2 bay leaves
2 cloves
½ onion, finely chopped
6 slices stale bread, crusts removed
½ tsp English mustard powder
salt and freshly ground black pepper

Method

- Put the milk, cream, bay leaves, cloves and onion in a medium-sized saucepan and simmer gently for 10 minutes. At the end of the cooking time, take the pan off the heat and remove the bay leaves and cloves.
- Break the bread into small pieces and add to the milk. Return the pan to the heat and simmer gently for about 5 minutes or until the bread has absorbed all the liquid, stirring occasionally.
- Add the mustard powder and season with salt and pepper. The finished sauce should have the consistency of porridge and will have a delicious creamy flavour.

Mint Sauce

There is nothing to compare with the taste of fresh mint sauce to go with your Sunday joint of roast lamb. It was a tradition with my family, and even today I always have a small patch of mint in the corner of my garden, contained in a bucket to curb its invasive habits.

Makes approximately 200 ml (7 fl oz)

50 g (2 oz) fresh mint leaves
2 tbsp white sugar
250 ml (8 fl oz) malt vinegar

Method

- Using a large-bladed knife, chop the mint until it is in tiny pieces. It helps if you sprinkle the leaves with a little sugar just before you start chopping.
- Put the vinegar in a small, stainless steel saucepan and bring to simmering point. Add the sugar and the mint and cook for about 20 minutes to allow the flavours to infuse.
- Pour the sauce into hot, sterilized jars and seal immediately.
- Mint sauce will store in the fridge for up to 6 months. Remember to shake well before serving as the mint will settle in the bottom of the jar.

Cranberry Sauce

Christmas dinner simply wouldn't be complete without some cranberry sauce to complement the flavour of the turkey.

Makes approximately 250 g (9 oz) jar

300 g (10 oz) fresh cranberries
zest and juice of 1 orange
120 g (4 oz) white granulated sugar

Method

- Wash the cranberries and place them in a large saucepan. Remove two pieces of zest from the orange with a vegetable peeler and then extract the juice. Add the juice and pieces of zest to the cranberries.
- Add the sugar and stir well.
- Place the saucepan on a medium heat and bring to a gentle boil, stirring occasionally to dissolve the sugar. Put the lid on the saucepan and simmer for about 20 minutes or until the cranberries have become soft.
- Taste to make sure that you are happy with the sweetness before bottling in a sterilized jar.

Making the Perfect Gravy

The quality of your gravy will depend on the quality of the juices left in your pan after roasting a joint of meat. Make sure you season the meat sufficiently and brown it on all sides before putting it into the oven. For even more flavour it is worth roasting some vegetables along with the meat. They will be overcooked so you will need to discard them, but they will give the sediment in the cooking pan a wonderful depth of flavour.

When the meat is cooked, remove it from the pan and leave to stand for 20 minutes before carving. Gently spoon off most of the fat from the surface of the meat juices left in the pan. Crush the vegetables with a fork and then strain the juices through a sieve. Pour the sieved juices back into the cooking pan and place it over a high heat. Make sure to scrape the sides with a wooden spoon to get all the goodness into the juices.

Next, add 1 tablespoon of plain flour and mix thoroughly to avoid it becoming lumpy. Next, using stock that you have made (see pages 11–15) gradually pour it into the meat pan, stirring all the time. Simmer for around 15 minutes or until the gravy starts to thicken. Taste and adjust the seasoning if necessary before serving.

Vegetables

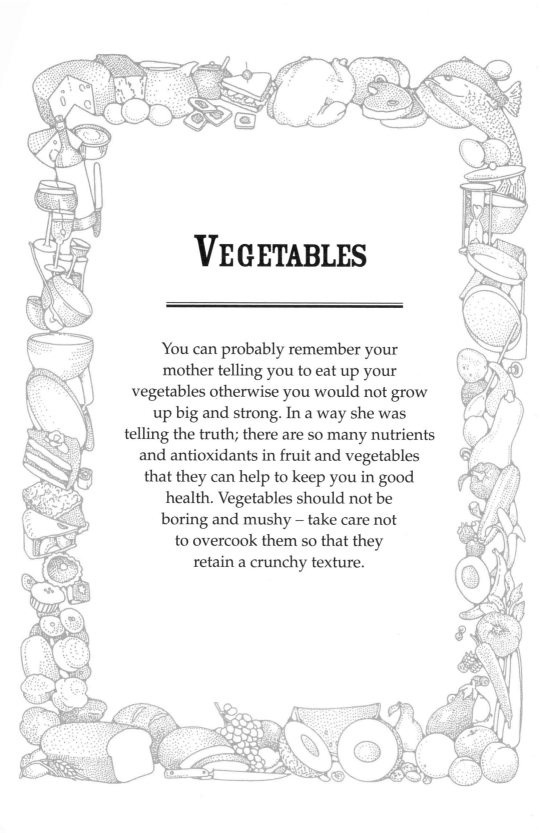

You can probably remember your mother telling you to eat up your vegetables otherwise you would not grow up big and strong. In a way she was telling the truth; there are so many nutrients and antioxidants in fruit and vegetables that they can help to keep you in good health. Vegetables should not be boring and mushy – take care not to overcook them so that they retain a crunchy texture.

Vegetables

If you do not have the luxury of a large garden or access to an allotment, this does not mean that you cannot grow your own vegetables. You really do not need lots of space, and learning which varieties grow well in containers and how to encourage them to produce the maximum crop will be a big help. Start off by planting fast-growing crops such as salad leaves, radishes and beetroot as they do not require much room and will grow quite happily among other plants. Do not bother to plant vegetables that you know you will not eat on a regular basis – it is a waste of space that could be used to grow your favourite foods.

If you only have a patio garden, containers such as windowboxes, buckets or even old tin baths all make suitable sites for vegetables as long as they are in a sunny position. Ask your local nursery to recommend dwarf varieties – you can still get a bumper crop and the quality of the vegetable will not be less good just because it is smaller. Tomatoes work very well in containers, especially the tumbler variety, and you can even grow them in hanging baskets in order to save on ground space. Prepare to be inventive and you will be surprised just how much you can grow.

You can buy bags of compost specially designed for vegetables and they will contain most of the nutrients your plants will need for their growing season. However, if possible, find room for a compost bin so that you can recycle your kitchen waste – it does not take long for it to turn into a wonderful, rich compost that you can use to put essential nutrients back into the soil.

Vegetables start to lose their natural sweetness within hours after harvesting, so pick only as much as you need, ideally as close to cooking time as possible. If you find you have a glut of a particular vegetable, as often happens, most can be stored by blanching them for a few minutes in boiling water, cooling them rapidly in iced water and then placing them in the freezer to use throughout the winter.

Asparagus and Egg Starter

Asparagus is prized for its delicate flavour and is best eaten within hours of being harvested. As it can be expensive to buy it is still considered to be a luxury, but it can be grown at home – though it does require plenty of space as it occupies a permanent spot.

Serves 4

450 g (1 lb) asparagus spears
2 eggs
50 g (2 oz) unsalted butter
1 tbsp flour
300 ml (10 fl oz) milk
50 g (2 oz) parmesan cheese
½ tsp smoked sweet paprika
salt and freshly ground black pepper
8 fresh anchovy fillets
4 sprigs of fresh parsley, to garnish

Method

- Wash the asparagus carefully so as not to damage the tender tips. Hold each spear in both hands and bend gently (the asparagus should snap where the woody part meets the tender tops). Discard the woody ends.
- Put the eggs in a pan of cold water, bring it to simmering point and cook them for 7 minutes to hard-boil them. Cool them rapidly under cold running water then transfer them to a pan of cold water until they are cool enough to handle. Remove the shells and slice the eggs.
- Make a white sauce by melting the butter in a saucepan. Remove the pan from the heat and stir in the flour. Slowly add the milk, whisking so that lumps do not form, then return the pan to the heat and gently bring to the boil, stirring continuously. Add the parmesan cheese and the paprika and cook until the sauce thickens. Season to taste with salt and pepper.

- Place the asparagus in a steamer and cook for 5 minutes, or cook in a pan of salted boiling water for 4 minutes. Drain and lay on 4 individual plates.
- Lay the slices of hard-boiled egg over the top of the asparagus and then lay 2 anchovy fillets on each plate on top of the egg. Pour the sauce over the top and dress with a sprig of fresh parsley. Serve immediately with a handful of parmesan crisps (see below).

Parmesan Crisps

These are so easy to make and yet totally irresistible. They do not keep well, so they are best eaten straight away.

Makes approximately 40 crisps

150 g (5 oz) parmesan cheese, finely grated
freshly ground black pepper

Method

- Preheat the oven to 170°C (325°F/Gas mark 3). Lay a sheet of greaseproof paper on a baking tray. Place a 5 cm (2 in) circular pastry cutter on the paper and sprinkle a heaped teaspoon of parmesan inside it to make a complete circle. There is no need to press the cheese down firmly as it will melt as it cooks.
- Gently move the cutter to a new position and repeat the process until you have used up all the cheese, making sure that you leave a space between each circle so that the crisps will be easy to remove once cooked. Sprinkle each crisp with a little black pepper.
- Cook in the oven until the cheese has melted and turned golden brown. You will need to watch the crisps carefully once they start to brown as they can quickly overcook.
- Gently remove each crisp from the greaseproof paper, using a fish slice or spatula, and cool on a wire rack until they are crisp.

Creamed Broad Beans and Bacon

This is a delightful way of serving broad beans. The recipe works best if the beans are picked while they are still young so that they retain their natural sweetness.

Serves 4

450 g (1 lb) broad beans, shelled
3 streaky bacon rashers, chopped
1 tbsp plain flour
10 g (¼ oz) butter
salt and freshly ground black pepper
75 ml (3 fl oz) double cream
chopped parsley, to garnish

Method

- ❖ Put the shelled beans in a pan of lightly salted boiling water. Cover the pan with a lid and cook for about 10 minutes or until the beans are tender. Drain the beans and reserve the cooking liquid.
- ❖ Fry the bacon in a dry frying pan until really crisp. Stir the flour into the bacon and cook for a few minutes. Add the butter and gradually stir in a little of the cooking liquid from the beans. Keep adding liquid until you have a creamy sauce, stirring continuously. Season with salt and pepper.
- ❖ Fold the drained beans into the sauce and then stir in the double cream. Heat gently and serve with a sprinkle of fresh parsley on top.

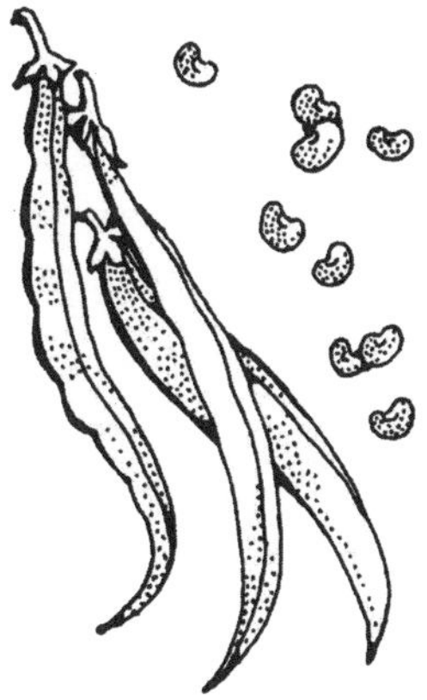

Cheesy French Beans

You can serve this as a supper dish on its own, or as an accompaniment to some thinly sliced boiled gammon. Try a few different cheeses – I find that Gruyère is a great alternative to Cheddar. This recipe also works well with young courgettes. Simply slice them in half, steam for about 5 minutes and then follow the recipe below.

Serves 4

450 g (1 lb) French beans
2 tbsp sunflower oil
1 garlic clove, halved
salt and freshly ground black pepper
75 g (3 oz) Cheddar cheese, thinly sliced or Gruyère
1 tsp smoked sweet paprika
2 fresh tomatoes, sliced
fresh chives, snipped

Method

- Preheat the oven to 190°C (375°F/Gas mark 5).
- Put the beans in a pan of lightly salted boiling water and cook for 5–7 minutes or until they are tender but still crunchy. Drain and then refresh them in cold water.
- Brush a baking tray with a little of the oil and rub the garlic clove all over the dish. This gives a hint of garlic without it overpowering the rest of the ingredients.
- Arrange the drained beans on the baking tray in a single layer. Brush them liberally with oil and then sprinkle with salt and pepper.
- Lay the cheese over the top of the beans. Sprinkle some smoked paprika over the cheese and then top with some slices of fresh tomato.
- Place in the preheated oven, near the top, and cook for 15–20 minutes or until the cheese has melted and is bubbling nicely. Sprinkle some freshly snipped chives over the top just before serving.

Roasted Winter Vegetables

This is probably the easiest way to cook winter vegetables as not only can you prepare them well in advance, they can be roasted all together in the same baking tray. They make a perfect side dish to accompany any roast meat or poultry and I can guarantee they will be a hit with your dinner guests. Just make sure that you cut the vegetables all the same size so that they cook evenly. Celeriac can discolour quite quickly once peeled and cut, so if you are preparing it ahead put it in a bowl of cold water with a little lemon juice. The weights given in this recipe apply after the vegetables have been prepared.

Serves 6–8

12 shallots or small onions, chopped
350 g (12 oz) butternut squash, chopped
350 g (12 oz) turnip, chopped
350 g (12 oz) parsnips, chopped
350 g (12 oz) celeriac, chopped
2 beetroot, peeled and chopped
4 medium carrots, chopped
8 small new potatoes, chopped
1 garlic clove, whole
1 tbsp fresh herbs such as rosemary, thyme or sage, finely chopped
salt and freshly ground black pepper
3 tbsp olive oil

Method

- Preheat the oven to 220°C (425°F/Gas mark 7. Just before you are ready to cook the vegetables, put them all in a large bowl, add the garlic, herbs, plenty of salt and black pepper and the olive oil and mix thoroughly with your hands until each piece is coated.
- Spread the vegetables out on a large baking tray and bake in the oven for 40–45 minutes until they are tender and just starting to brown at the edges.

Beetroot and Apple Salad

This is a sharp, tangy salad with a great combination of flavours. It is very quick to prepare as it requires no cooking and works very well with cold fish or meats (particularly pork) for a summer lunch.

Serves 4

3 uncooked beetroot, peeled and grated
2 large eating apples, peeled, cored and grated
150 ml (¼ pint) sour cream
2 tsp lemon juice
1 tsp sugar
salt and freshly ground black pepper
75 ml (3 fl oz) whipping cream

Method

- Put the grated beetroot and apple into a large bowl and add the sour cream, lemon juice, sugar and salt and pepper. Mix the ingredients together to combine thoroughly.
- Whip the cream until it forms soft peaks and then fold into the beetroot and apple salad.

Crispy-topped Broccoli

This is a different way of serving broccoli as it has a crispy topping of breadcrumbs and cheese. It goes well with any type of fish and is also a great accompaniment to chicken.

Serves 4

450 g (1 lb) broccoli spears
salt and freshly ground black pepper

300 ml (10 fl oz) white sauce (see page 31)
50 g (2 oz) unsalted butter
3 tbsp white breadcrumbs
3 tbsp Cheddar cheese, grated

Method

- Cook the broccoli spears by steaming them for approximately 6 minutes or puttng them in lightly salted boiling water for 5 minutes, until the stalks are just tender but not soft. Drain thoroughly and arrange them in the bottom of an ovenproof dish.
- Make the white sauce and spoon it over the broccoli.
- Preheat the grill to hot. Melt the butter in a saucepan and then stir in the breadcrumbs until all the butter has been absorbed. Remove from the heat, allow to cool slightly and then mix the grated cheese into the breadcrumbs mixture. Add a generous grinding of black pepper.
- Sprinkle the breadcrumb mixture over the top of the white sauce and place the dish under the grill for a few minutes to give it a golden-brown finish.

Pease Pudding

If you want something really traditional to go with some boiled ham, why not try this simple recipe using split peas.

Serves 6

450 g (1 lb) yellow split peas
1 onion, finely chopped
600 ml (1 pint) water saved from boiling the ham
salt and freshly ground black pepper

Method

- Cover the split peas with water in a large bowl and allow to soak overnight.

- Drain the peas and put them in a saucepan with the chopped onion and water reserved from boiling the ham.
- Bring to the boil, cover, reduce the heat and simmer until the peas are tender. If they start to look dry add a little more water to keep them moist.
- Once tender, put the peas in a blender and whizz until you have a smooth paste. Season to taste and then put the peas into a greased oven dish. Bake in a preheated oven at 180°C (350°F/Gas mark 4) for 30 minutes.

Sprouts with Bacon and Chestnuts

The younger members of my family used to pull a face if I served up Brussels sprouts with roast dinner, but they changed their opinion when I experimented one Christmas – not a single one was left on their plates. The secret to serving Brussels sprouts is not to overcook them, then they remain slightly crunchy and the flavour is not quite so strong.

Serves 4

350 g (12 oz) Brussels sprouts
4 rashers of smoked streaky bacon
175 g (6 oz) chestnuts, cooked and shells removed
50 g (2 oz) unsalted butter
freshly ground black pepper

Method

- Remove the outer leaves from the Brussels sprouts and cut them in half. Steam for about 4 minutes or until they are lightly cooked but still crunchy.
- Cut the streaky bacon up into tiny pieces and fry in a dry frying pan until they are really crispy. Remove from the pan and set aside.
- Cut the cooked chestnuts into fairly small pieces and set aside.
- Melt the butter in the same frying pan in which you cooked the bacon and then add the sprouts, bacon and chestnuts and freshly ground black pepper. Shake the pan until all the sprouts are coated in butter and serve.

Stuffed Cabbage

This is a hearty meal in itself and a recipe that is well worth trying. You can experiment with different fillings until you find the one that suits you best.

Serves 4

225 g (8 oz) cooked ham, finely chopped or minced
225 g (8 oz) cooked pork, finely chopped or minced
1 garlic clove, finely chopped
1 onion, finely chopped
2 tbsp white breadcrumbs
6 chestnut mushrooms, finely chopped
bunch of fresh sage, finely chopped
1 tsp ground cumin
1 tsp ground coriander
1 tbsp plain flour
salt and freshly ground black pepper
1 egg, beaten
450 ml (15 fl oz) milk
1 medium-sized white cabbage

Method

- Prepare the stuffing by mixing together the ham, pork, garlic, onion, breadcrumbs, chestnut mushrooms, sage and spices. Once they are thoroughly combined, add the flour and season with salt and pepper. Beat together the egg and the milk and then gradually add to the stuffing mixture until it reaches a firm consistency and holds together when pressed between the hands.
- Remove the tough outer leaves from the cabbage, trim off the stalk and then slice off the top and put to one side. Scoop out the middle from the cabbage using a sharp knife and a spoon, leaving a shell that is at least 2.5 cm (1 in) thick.
- Press the stuffing in the middle of the cabbage, replace the lid and hold

in place by tying a piece of kitchen string around the cabbage. Wrap the cabbage in kitchen foil and fold over the top to form a complete parcel.
- Place the foil parcel in a large saucepan and gently pour in boiling water at the side until it comes about two-thirds of the way up the parcel.
- Cook for 1½ hours or until the cabbage is tender and the stuffing is cooked.
- Turn the cabbage out onto a serving plate and serve with a white sauce poured over the top (see page 31).

Honey-glazed Baby Carrots

Honey brings out the natural sweetness in baby carrots and they taste superb when served with grilled or roasted meat and poultry, or even white fish.

Serves 4

450 g (1 lb) baby carrots
salt and freshly ground black pepper
25 g (1 oz) unsalted butter
2 tbsp clear honey
½ tsp ground cinnamon
¼ tsp ground nutmeg
fresh parsley, to garnish

Method

- Leave the baby carrots whole unless they are fairly large, in which case slice them in half lengthways. Cook them in a pan of lightly salted boiling water for about 10 minutes until they are tender but still retain a crunch.
- Melt the butter in another pan, add the honey and stir until it has melted. Toss the carrots in the butter mixture until they are evenly coated and just starting to turn light brown.
- Serve sprinkled with the cinnamon and nutmeg and fresh parsley.

Braised Celery

Celery is not much used as a cooked vegetable these days, but braised in this way it goes really well with roasted or grilled meat and fish.

Serves 4

2 celery heads
salt and freshly ground black pepper
1 small onion, thinly sliced
2 baby carrots, thinly sliced
300 ml (10 fl oz) chicken stock (see pages 11–12)
25 g (1 oz) plain flour
25 g (1 oz) unsalted butter

Method

- Trim the roots from the celery, along with any leaves and damaged stems. Scrub well under cold running water and cut in half lengthways.
- Cook the celery in slightly salted boiling water for about 10 minutes and drain well.
- Place the celery in an flameproof dish and cover with the onion and carrot.
- Pour the stock over and season well with salt and pepper. Cover with a lid and cook gently for about 45 minutes over a low heat.
- Knead together the flour and the butter and add to the braising liquid in small pieces. Simmer for a further 5 minutes to cook the flour, when the stock should have thickened nicely.

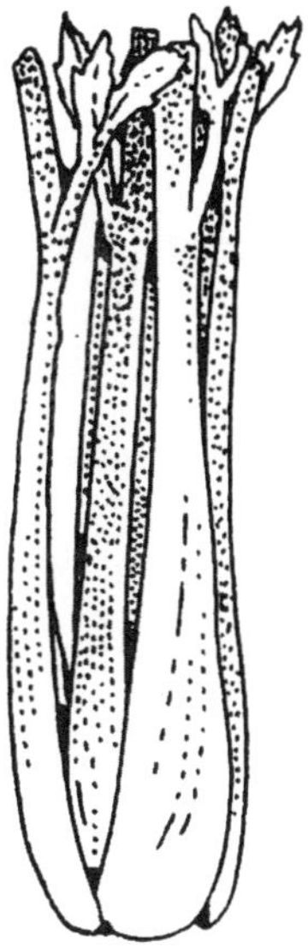

Kale and Potato Cakes

These great little potato patties are really good served with sausages instead of the usual mash, or try them with some boiled gammon and pineapple.

Serves 4

225 g (8 oz) kale
salt and freshly ground black pepper
450 g (1 lb) potatoes, cubed
2 eggs, beaten
50 g (2 oz) wholemeal breadcrumbs
50 g (2 oz) unsalted butter

Method

- Shred the kale finely, discarding any thick stalks. Blanch in lightly salted boiling water for 2 minutes and then drain thoroughly in a colander.
- Boil the potatoes in lightly salted water until they are soft and then mash using a fork or a potato masher.
- Combine the kale and potatoes and then blend in the beaten eggs and the breadcrumbs until the mixture reaches a fairly stiff consistency. Season well with salt and black pepper and then shape into balls about the size of an egg. Press the balls flat with the palm of your hand so that you have a flat patty shape.
- Melt the butter in a large frying pan and fry the potato cakes until they are brown on both sides.

Perfect Potatoes

Mashed potato is a classic comfort food when you are feeling a little under the weather, but it can be unpleasant if it turns out lumpy. The secret is really in your choice of potato (Desirée or Maris Piper are the preferred varieties) and in making sure they are cooked fully before mashing. Quantities are not given for this recipe as it will depend on the amount of people you are feeding, but allow 1 medium-sized potato per person.

- Peel your potatoes and cut them into equal-sized pieces so that they will all be cooked at the same time. Rinse thoroughly in cold water to remove any excess starch.

- Place the potatoes in a saucepan with enough lightly salted cold water to cover them. Bring to the boil and continue to cook for 15–20 minutes until a knife goes through them easily. When they are cooked, drain them in a colander and leave to sit for a few minutes until all the water has drained away.

- Put the potatoes back into the saucepan or into a large bowl. Add 25 g (1 oz) butter and a little single cream (about 1 tablespoon) and start to mash. You can do this using a fork, but a potato masher will make the job a little easier. Keep adding the cream a little at a time until you have a thick, creamy consistency. Finish by adding freshly ground black pepper and a little grated nutmeg.

The secret of the perfect roast potato is really hot fat and parboiling the potatoes until they are fluffy on the outside but not cooked all the way through.

- Peel and cut the potatoes into even-sized pieces and rinse off any excess starch under cold water. Boil for about 10 minutes and test with a fork to see if the outside layer is cooked.

- Preheat lard or goose fat in a baking tray at the top of the oven at 220°C (425°F/Gas mark 7). Drain the potatoes and, putting the lid back on the saucepan, shake vigorously to fluff up their surface. Carefully place the potatoes in the hot fat using a slotted spoon and roast in the oven for about 40–45 minutes until they are golden brown and crispy.

Pickling and Preserving

In my grandmother's day, before the era of modern conveniences such as freezers and fridges, foods were pickled or preserved in some way to make them last longer. Today we eat pickles and chutneys just because we like the different flavours they offer. I am giving you a couple of my favourite recipes – ones that you can use at any time of the year to accompany cold meats, barbecues or picnics.

Pickled Onions

This traditional recipe can also be used to make pickled gherkins (or baby cucumbers) and beetroot.

Makes 4 jars

1 kg (2¼ lb) pickling onions or shallots, peeled and trimmed
50 g (2 oz) sea salt
2 chillies
1.2 litres (2 pints) white wine vinegar
200 g (7 oz) light brown sugar
1 tbsp mustard seeds
1 small cinnamon stick
1 bay leaf

Method

- Place the onions in a bowl, sprinkle with salt, then cover and leave overnight.
- The next morning rinse and dry the onions with some kitchen paper. Put them into warm, sterilized jars with half a chilli in each jar.

❖ Boil the vinegar, sugar, spices and bay leaf for 1 minute and then pour over the top of the onions in each of the jars. Seal and leave for at least 4 weeks before opening.

Tomato and Chilli Chutney

This is by far the easiest tomato chutney I have ever made and it has a wonderful natural flavour that is not too sweet. It goes really well with cheese and cold meats and is great for using up the glut of tomatoes at the end of the growing season.

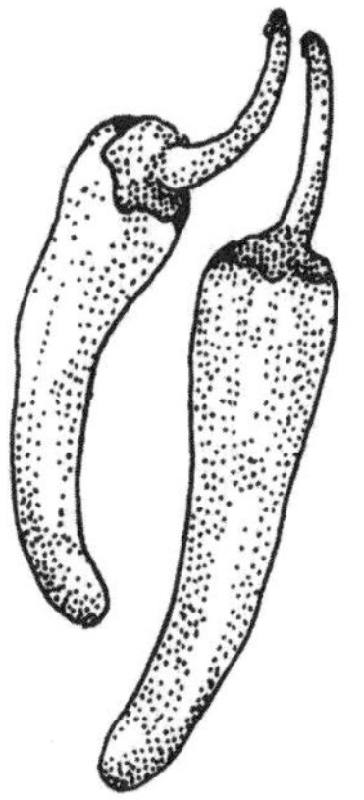

Makes 4 jars

6 red chillies (whole)
450 g (1 lb) tomatoes, finely chopped
1 green pepper, finely chopped
2 garlic cloves, crushed
1 thumb-sized piece of gingerroot, grated
150 g (5 oz) light brown sugar
100 ml (3½ fl oz) red wine vinegar

Method

❖ Put the chillies, tomatoes and pepper into a large, heavy-based saucepan. Add the garlic, ginger, sugar and vinegar and bring to the boil. Reduce the heat and simmer for about 1 hour, stirring from time to time.

❖ Pour into warm, sterilized jars and seal while still hot. Leave these for at least 1 month before opening so that the flavours can infuse.

HERBS

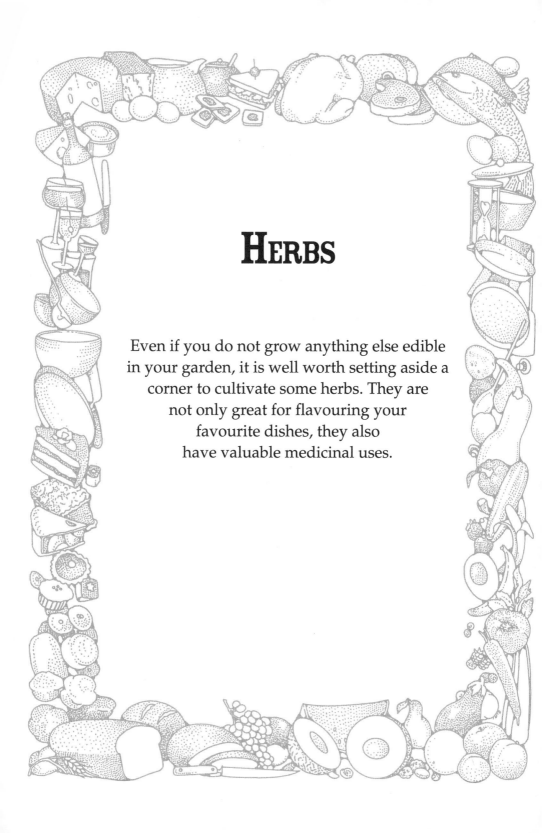

Even if you do not grow anything else edible in your garden, it is well worth setting aside a corner to cultivate some herbs. They are not only great for flavouring your favourite dishes, they also have valuable medicinal uses.

The Benefits of Herbs

If you have no space in your flower beds herbs will grow quite happily in pots as long as you remember to water them regularly, and occasionally give them a boost with a little plant food. By regularly picking your herbs you should have an ample supply that will see you through the year. You can also grow some indoors on your kitchen windowsill when the weather turns cold so that you always have a fresh supply. You will never return to those little pots of dried herbs once you have tasted fresh ones, though it is useful to dry some of your own for use during the winter months.

HOW TO DRY HERBS

By far the best way of drying herbs is to let them dry naturally in the air; this slow process means they will retain the maximum amount of their beneficial oils. Herbs used for their foliage should be harvested before they flower. Pick your herbs in the morning, after any dew has dried but before the day becomes hot, and only cut healthy sprigs, making sure you remove any dry or diseased leaves. Now follow these simple steps:

- Shake the herbs to remove any insects and then wash gently in cold water. Pat them with some kitchen paper to remove the excess moisture and leave to dry thoroughly.
- You need the bottom stems of the herbs free so that you can tie them together, so remove any leaves on the bottom 2.5 cm (1 in) of stem.
- Next, you need some kitchen string or garden twine so that you can tie 3–4 sprigs of each herb together in a small bundle. If you do not have any string handy you can always use a rubber band.
- Take a brown paper bag that is large enough to hold one bundle, and make a few holes in the paper to allow air to circulate.
- Before placing the herbs inside the bag, make a clear label of the herb you are drying and the date it was put inside the bag.

- Place the bundle of herbs upside down inside the bag and gather the ends of the bag around the stalks. Make sure that the herbs are not too crowded otherwise there will be no room for air to circulate and they will go mouldy. Tie the bag closed with string or a rubber band, leaving a loop from which to hang it upside down in an airy room.
- Check the herbs in a couple of weeks. When they are dry and crumbly, take them out of the bag and put them into containers or plastic bags for storage.

HEALING PROPERTIES

While herbs are invaluable for culinary reasons, many of these aromatic plants have medicinal properties and can be used instead of some of the

Herb Hints

- Make sure you clearly label the storage jars or plastic bags before putting them away.
- Throw away any herbs that show the slightest sign of mould.
- Dry herbs whole and crush them when you are ready to use them, as this way they will retain their maximum flavour.
- Fill the containers right to the top to minimize the oxygen around the stored herbs. Transfer them to smaller containers as you use them up.
- Keep your containers away from direct sunlight in a cool, dry place as light, heat and oxygen are enemies to dried herbs and will destroy their potency.
- Use your dried herbs within a year as they will start to lose their flavour and beneficial oils after this time.
- Dried herbs are stronger than fresh ones – 1 teaspoon of dried is equivalent to 1 tablespoon of fresh.

strong over-the-counter remedies. Remember, though, you should consult your doctor before embarking on any kind of self-medication, especially if you are already taking prescribed drugs. Also, it is not recommended that you use any of these remedies on very young children or if you are pregnant. Always seek medical advice if you are not sure.

Basil This pungent herb is a natural fly and mosquito repellent, so it is worth growing some close to the house or even on the windowsill. Basil is a member of the mint family and is rich in vitamin K, iron and calcium. It is

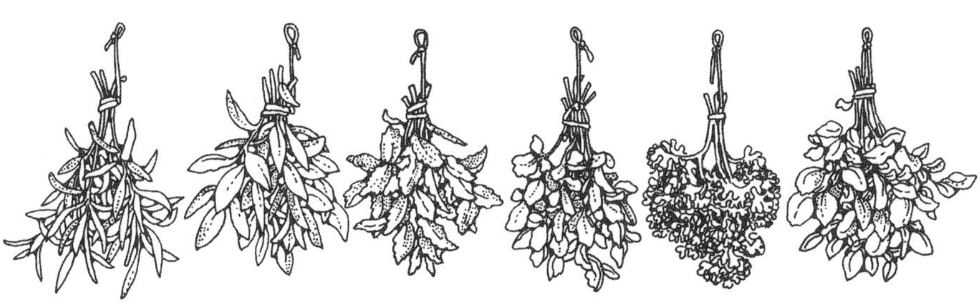

generally used for its digestive properties, so drinking a cup of basil tea can aid digestion and prevent a build-up of wind. Simply infuse a few leaves in a cup of boiling water and then drink the tea hot or cold as you prefer. It can also be used to treat bad breath, stomach cramps, nausea, vomiting, headaches and, because it has mild sedative properties, anxiety.

Chives This herb is exceptionally easy to grow and belongs to the same family as garlic, onions and leeks, which are renowned for their cancer-fighting properties and treatment of high blood pressure. Chives can also be used to ease upset stomachs as they help to stimulate the appetite and, if chewed, can help to relieve a sore throat. They are rich in folic acid and so, eaten regularly, can help to keep your heart healthy.

Coriander A rich source of iron and magnesium, coriander can also help to lower cholesterol if eaten on a regular basis. It can be used regularly in your diet or drunk as a herbal tea in the same way as basil. It is also believed to help relieve the swelling associated with arthritis and rheumatism, as it has natural anti-inflammatory properties. It has antibacterial properties which can help to destroy the bacteria that causes diarrhoea and other stomach disorders, combined with a muscle relaxant to take away stomach cramps.

Dill This is a very pungent herb which is usually associated with digestive disorders as it stimulates the secretion of bile and other digestive juices. Dill can also help in the relief of hiccups and has a calming effect which can help you get a good night's sleep. Because the essential oils found in dill are both germicidal and antioxidants, chewing this herb can help to relieve the symptoms of bad breath, or it can be taken as a tea.

Fennel Fennel is another herb that is good at treating indigestion or an upset stomach. Both the seeds and herbs can be used. Chewing fennel seeds after a meal can help aid digestion and also freshen the breath. It is probably most popular as an anti-flatulent as it can quickly expel wind from the stomachs of both young and old. Fennel can also act as a diuretic, helping to dispel toxic substances from the body by encouraging more frequent urination. Taken regularly as a tea, it is said to sharpen the memory and relax the body in times of stress.

Garlic Although this is generally regarded as a vegetable rather than a herb, it gains a place here because of its medicinal benefits. A compound called allicin, which is released when a garlic clove is crushed or cut and gives garlic its characteristic taste and smell, is considered to be responsible for its therapeutic qualities. Recent research has proved that if garlic is eaten on a regular basis it can help to ward off colds. If that is not enough reason for including it in your diet, then consider that it also boosts your body's supply of vitamins A, B and C. Garlic is also believed to be beneficial in fighting heart disease, lowering blood pressure and helping to maintain a healthy level of cholesterol. Scientists are researching the benefits of garlic as its antibacterial effects were discovered early in the 19th century after an outbreak of a fever that spread quickly throughout Europe; it was found that those people who included garlic in their diet on a regular basis remained healthy. It is not necessary to chew garlic cloves to gain their benefits – just remember to use a couple of cloves in your everyday recipes and that will be enough to help ward off infections.

Mint A herb that is enjoyed as a tea in many parts of the world because it is well known for its ability to settle digestive problems, including the discomfort of irritable bowel syndrome, and to slow the growth of some of the harmful bacteria found in the gut. When you make your mint tea, always cover the pot while the tea is infusing otherwise many of the beneficial oils will be lost in the steam. Mint also works well in the treatment of nausea and headaches. Simply crush a few leaves in your hand and breathe in the oil that is released, or drink some hot mint tea. It can also be used as an inhalant to help relieve the congestion associated with a cold. Finally, with its germicidal properties, mint can help inhibit harmful bacteria from forming inside the mouth by cleaning the tongue and teeth, leaving you with fresh-smelling breath.

Oregano This makes a wonderful tea which, if taken regularly, is believed to help slow down the ageing process, improving the flexibility of joints and muscles. It is also rich in antioxidants and antibacterial properties, and is thought to help strengthen the body's immune system. It is useful in aiding digestive problems and, if used as an oil, can help to treat itchy skin and some skin infections.

Parsley Probably best known as a source of chlorophyll which is great at eliminating bad breath, parsley is also rich in zinc and contains more vitamin C than any other fruit or vegetable. Eating fresh parsley is by far the best way to get the benefits from this herb, but you can make a herbal drink by liquidizing the leaves with some water. Parsley acts as a diuretic, is said to improve the aches and pains associated with rheumatism, and is also an appetite stimulant.

Sage The most common medicinal use of sage is as a mouthwash to treat sore throats and inflammation of the mouth and gums. To make the mouthwash, add a tablespoon of crushed sage leaves to a cup of boiling water, strain after 10 minutes and then leave the mixture to cool to room temperature. Sage also works well as a compress to help soothe the pain and swelling of sprains and strains. Sage tea aids digestive problems and works as a mild laxative.

Tarragon This herb has been used for its medicinal qualities for centuries as it has the ability to numb the mouth when chewed. For many years it was used as a treatment for toothache and also as an antidote against poisonous snake bites. Today, it is more commonly used to stimulate the appetite after a period of illness and can help in relieving stomach cramps. Tarragon can also act as a mild sedative, helping to give you a good night's sleep. To obtain the calming benefits of tarragon, put a tablespoon of crushed leaves into a cup of boiling water and leave to infuse for about 10 minutes.

Thyme Another age-old cure for many ailments, thyme has powerful antiseptic properties. Taken as a tea infusion, it can help to relieve breathing problems associated with colds, influenza or bronchitis and is particularly effective for soothing throat infections. The same infusion can be applied to a cotton wool pad and placed on the eyes to treat conjunctivitis and styes. Thyme is also beneficial in aiding the digestion of food and can considerably soothe the symptoms of gastroenteritis. To prepare thyme tea, crush about 6 leaves into half a cup of boiling water and allow to steep for 10–15 minutes. To make the tea more palatable, add a teaspoon of honey. Thyme tea is also very good at relieving uncomfortable menstrual cramps.

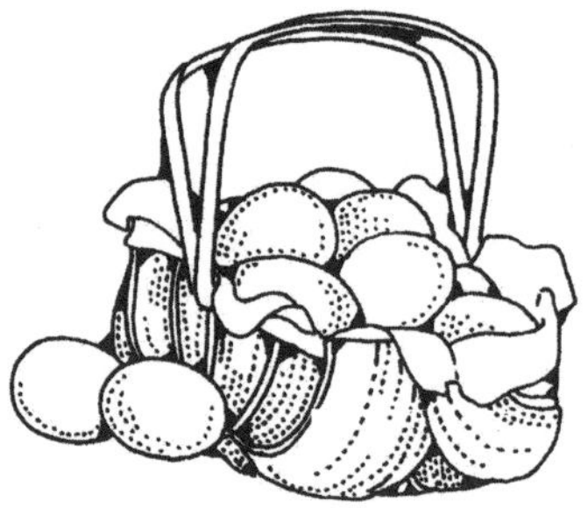

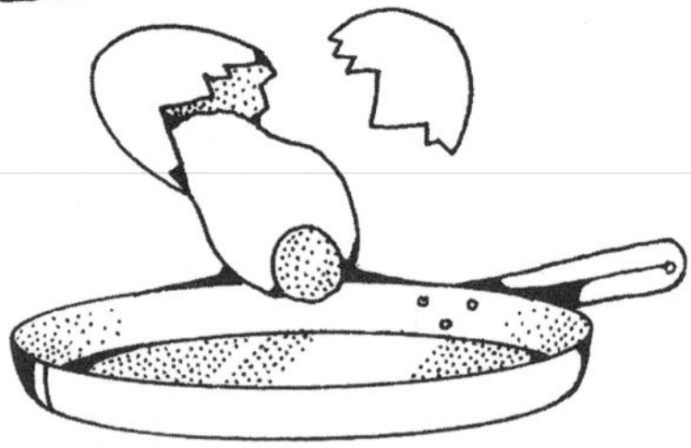

Eggs

Eggs are one of the most nutritious items in our diet and really a complete meal in themselves. They are rich in minerals, proteins and vitamins, all of which are easily absorbed by the body, making them easy to digest.

Cooking Eggs

Giving instructions for basic ways of cooking eggs might seem unnecessary, but there is an art to getting them just right every time. Have you ever looked forward to a breakfast boiled egg with a nice runny yolk to dip your toast 'soldiers' in only to find you have over- or undercooked it? Making the perfect boiled egg is not something everyone knows how to do.

Follow my simple instructions and you will always have the perfect boiled egg with a nice runny yolk but a firm white, too, without any of those stringy bits that often put people off. I have included other simple egg recipes here just to show how versatile this little food package can be.

The Perfect Boiled Egg

- Put about 5 cm (2 in) of boiling water from a kettle into a small saucepan and place it on the hob on a high setting. Bring the water back to the boil and carefully transfer the egg into the saucepan without dropping it, using a long-handled spoon. As soon as the water starts to boil again, set your timer for 4 minutes. While the eggs are cooking you should have just enough time to make your 'soldiers'.
- As soon as the timer goes off, lift the egg out of the water using a slotted spoon and place it into an eggcup. Gently tap the top of the egg until it cracks as this stops it from cooking any further. The egg should have a white that is completely set and a nice runny yolk for dipping your 'soldiers' into.

The timing given here is for eggs that have been kept at room temperature. Cooking boiled eggs straight from the fridge is not advisable as the shells are likely to crack as soon as they hit the hot water.

Scrambled Eggs

Some recipes for scrambled eggs advise whisking the eggs before cooking so that you incorporate some air, others simply add them to the pan whole and mix them while they cook. For light, fluffy scrambled eggs I find the following method never fails.

Serves 2

3 eggs
salt and pepper to taste
2 tbsp water
25 g (1 oz) butter
1 tbsp crème fraîche

Method

- Break the eggs into a clean mixing bowl, season with salt and pepper and then add the cold water. Whisk the eggs in an elliptical motion so that the yolks and whites are blended and you incorporate some air into the mixture.
- Melt the butter in a non-stick frying pan over a medium heat, taking care that it does not burn. Do not be tempted to turn up the heat in the pan, otherwise your eggs will cook too fast.
- When the butter has melted, add the beaten eggs to the pan. Leave them to cook for a minute and as they start to set, gently move them around so that they cook evenly. (Remember that metal objects will scratch a non-stick pan – I recommend that you use a silicon spatula.) Keep moving them slowly around the pan to avoid them becoming overcooked in places.
- Once the eggs are thickened but still soft, remove the pan from the heat, stir in the crème fraîche and transfer the eggs to a serving plate.

Poached Eggs

The secret to really successful poached eggs is to make sure that your eggs are very fresh – no older than four days. If you are lucky enough to have your own hens this will not be a problem, but if you have to buy your eggs, obtain them from a local farm if possible so you know exactly when they were laid. The method below is the way my grandmother cooked her poached eggs and I have followed her example for years with very good results. Some cooks say you should boil the water rapidly and swirl it before you put the eggs in, but my method is to keep the heat at medium and cook them more gently. The whites will be perfectly firm, yet the yolks will still be runny.

Method

- Place a frying pan over a medium heat and add boiling water from the kettle so that it fills the pan to a depth of about 2.5 cm (1 in).
- Put 1 teaspoon of white vinegar into the water and heat until there are just a few tiny bubbles starting to form over the bottom of the frying pan.
- Instead of cracking the egg straight into the pan, break it into a small bowl or cup first. This way there is no risk of getting pieces of shell mixed in with your egg. Do not turn up the heat – allow the egg to simmer gently without covering for 1 minute. Make sure you set your timer as it is very difficult to guess an exact minute.
- Now remove the pan from the heat and leave the egg to sit in the hot water for another 10 minutes (once again using your timer).
- When the timer pings, gently coax the egg from the pan using a slotted spoon. Rest the spoon on some folded kitchen paper for a few seconds to allow the excess water to drain away from the egg.
- Now serve your poached egg in your favourite way – on toast, on top of some freshly cut ham or maybe with some smoked haddock.

Fried Eggs

You might think that frying an egg is the simplest job in the kitchen, but there are many things that can go wrong. The most common mistake is trying to fry an egg that has come straight from the fridge – not only will it be too cold and make the fat in the pan spit, the egg will also spread all over the pan. Putting too much oil in the pan is another error; you need only a tiny amount of grease the bottom. Finally, take care that the pan is not too hot as it will cook the egg far too quickly and leave it crispy on the underside.

Method

- ❖ Remove the egg from the fridge at least 1 hour before you intend to use it.
- ❖ Add a little oil to a non-stick frying pan and bring it up to a medium heat.
- ❖ Crack the egg into a small bowl or cup first.
- ❖ When the pan has reached the correct heat, gently tip the egg into the centre of the pan. Gently fry for about 2 minutes. If you prefer your egg cooked on both sides, gently turn it over using a fish slice and cook for a further minute on the other side.
- ❖ Carefully remove the egg from the pan with your fish slice and serve as required.

Savoury Omelette

There are many versions of how to make the perfect omelette. Some chefs hold that the eggs should be beaten before putting them in the pan, while others prefer to mix them once they have started cooking. I am sure all the suggested methods work well, but I prefer my old and tested method that produces omelettes that always seem to turn out light and fluffy. The recipe that follows is for a plain omelette, but you can add any ingredients you like such as grated cheese, chopped ham or spicy sausage.

Serves 1

2 eggs
1 tbsp cold water
salt and freshly ground black pepper
25 g (1 oz) butter

Method

- Break the eggs into a bowl, add the water and season with salt and pepper. Whisk until the eggs are thoroughly mixed, but do not overwork as you do not want to get to the stage where the mixture becomes frothy.
- Melt the butter in a frying pan over medium heat. Once the butter is melted, but not browned, gently pour in the beaten egg so that it covers the bottom of the pan.
- Leave to cook on a medium heat for a couple of minutes. As the omelette starts to set around the outside, gently lift the edges using a spatula so that the uncooked egg can run beneath and cook on the hot surface of the pan.
- When the omelette is almost set but there is still a little runny egg on top, run your spatula underneath and gently fold the omelette in half. Slide it onto a warmed serving plate.

Perfect Pancakes

As children we never let Shrove Tuesday go by without nagging Grandmother to cook us some pancakes. She usually grumbled a little at this request, but she never failed to turn out a lovely pile of golden pancakes which we all tucked into with a generous helping of golden syrup and lemon juice. The pan needs to be smoking hot for pancakes so they cook rapidly on one side before being tossed over to finish the cooking.

Makes 6 pancakes

115 g (4 oz) plain flour
pinch of salt

1 egg
250 ml (8 fl oz) half milk/half water
50 g (2 oz) unsalted butter, melted
90 ml (3 fl oz) vegetable oil

Method

- Put the flour into a bowl, add a pinch of salt and make a well in the centre. Break the egg into the well, then add a little of the milk and water mixture and start to gradually combine to form a smooth paste.
- Beat in the remaining milk and water mixture little by little until you have a consistency that resembles single cream. When you are happy that you have the right consistency, add half the melted butter and stir to combine.
- Put your frying pan over a high heat and add a little butter with a teaspoon of cooking oil to prevent the butter from burning. When the pan is really hot, ladle about 3 tablespoons of the batter into the pan and quickly tip the frying pan so that the mixture covers the base evenly.
- When the edges of the pancake start to look brown and crisp you can either flip it over using a spatula to cook the other side, or you can have a go at tossing it. To do this, loosen the pancake with a spatula so that it slides freely over the bottom of the pan. Hold the handle in both hands and then jerk the pan forwards, at the same time tipping it slightly towards you. This action should cause the pancake to flip over and drop back into the pan (if you are lucky!) You might find you need to practise a few times before you get it right.
- Remember to re-grease the pan in between each pancake and continue until you have used up all the mixture. If you want to serve all the pancakes together, you can keep them hot in the oven with a layer of greaseproof paper between each one. Otherwise, serve them straight from the pan.

Magnificent Meringues

I used to shy away from cooking meringues, believing that they were really difficult to make. However, Grandmother taught me that as long as you follow a few simple rules they are one of the simplest desserts to make.

Simple Rules for Making Meringue

- Make sure all your equipment is squeaky clean before you start – even the tiniest speck of grease will stop your egg whites from forming stiff peaks.
- Add a little vinegar or lemon juice to your mixture after the addition of the sugar.
- Always use caster sugar, not granulated sugar, so that the meringue does not become gritty. Using golden unrefined caster sugar provides a slight flavour of caramel.
- An oven with a lowest setting of 60–70°C (140–158°F) is the ideal, but if yours does not have that, use the lowest temperature available. Your aim is to dry out the egg whites, not cook them, so you will need to prepare them when you do not require the oven for something else.

Makes 10 individual meringues

300 g (10 oz) caster sugar
5 egg whites (at room temperature)
1 tsp lemon juice

Method

- Turn your oven on to its lowest setting possible.
- Put the egg whites into a really clean bowl. Using an electric hand whisk or

a food processor with a whisk attachment, whisk until they start to froth.

- Gradually add the sugar to the egg whites, continuing to whisk meanwhile. Keep whisking until all the sugar has dissolved; you can test by running a little of the meringue through your fingers. Whisk until stiff peaks form and the egg white appears glossy. Add the lemon juice and whisk again.
- Line a baking tray with greaseproof paper and spoon the meringue onto the tray, making small rounds or one large one to make a pavlova.
- Place the baking tray near the bottom of the oven and bake until the outside of the meringue is crisp and it sounds hollow if you tap it on the bottom. You will need to be patient, as this can take several hours.

Yorkshire Puddings

The secret of really light, puffed-up Yorkshire puddings is first to make sure your fat is really hot before putting the batter in, and secondly never to be tempted to open the oven door halfway through cooking as this will make them sink as the cooler air hits them.

Makes 12 individual puddings

115 g (4 oz) plain flour
pinch of salt
1 egg, beaten
150 ml (5 fl oz) milk

Method

- Preheat the oven to 220°C (425°F/Gas mark 7). Sift the flour into a bowl and add a pinch of salt. Make a well in the middle, add the beaten egg and milk and whisk until a thick batter is formed. Leave the batter to stand in the fridge for 15 minutes.
- Put a small knob of lard into each compartment of a patty tin and place in the top of the oven. Once the fat is smoking hot, pour in the batter and cook for 20 minutes or until the puddings are risen and golden brown.

Fish

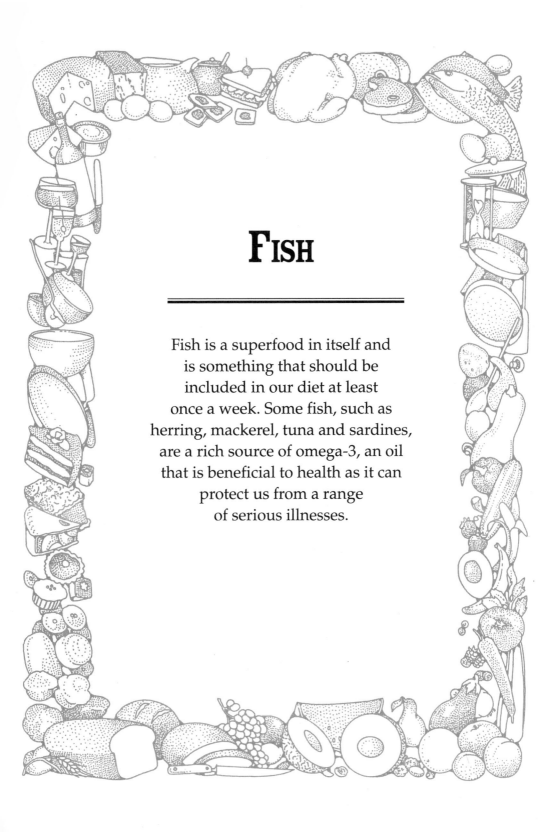

Fish is a superfood in itself and is something that should be included in our diet at least once a week. Some fish, such as herring, mackerel, tuna and sardines, are a rich source of omega-3, an oil that is beneficial to health as it can protect us from a range of serious illnesses.

Cooking Fish

If you are not lucky enough to live by the coast or know someone that regularly goes fishing, you will need to rely on your local fishmonger or supermarket for your supply of fish. Of course you will never really know exactly when the fish was caught, but if you follow these few simple tips you can be pretty certain that what you are buying is not past its best. This is particularly important when buying any type of seafood.

- Look at the eyes – they should be bright and clear. If they look grey and dull then the fish is past its prime.
- The skin of the fish should be shiny and appear almost metallic. If it is dull or has discoloured patches on it, do not risk buying the fish.
- Really fresh fish should not smell 'fishy' but rather have the smell of clean seawater.
- The gills should be a rich red in colour. If the fish is not fresh they will turn a much darker red.
- If you are unsure whether shrimp or prawns are totally fresh, it is best to buy frozen instead as the shell protects them from the rigours of the freezing process and, when thawed, they will still be packed with flavour.

Oily fish can help to reduce the risk of heart problems by lowering the 'bad' fats that build up in our bodies, so it is no wonder that doctors try to encourage us to eat more of this healthy food. All fish, including shellfish, are packed with various vitamins and minerals and they help to maintain healthy skin and keep joints supple, reducing the risk of arthritis.

Fish is really easy to cook and can be prepared in so many different ways. It can be grilled, fried, steamed, baked, poached, stewed, sautéed, stir-fried or cooked in its own little parcel of parchment or kitchen foil. Fish is one of the few foods that cooks successfully in a microwave, although of course this luxury was not available to our grandmothers.

Fish Pie

You can choose any fish to go in fish pie, so you do not need to follow my recipe exactly. However, the addition of some smoked fish greatly improves the flavour. I make my sauce by combining cream with the liquor the fish is poached in, which gives a rich, creamy texture and adds a touch of luxury.

Serves 4

150 ml (5 fl oz) milk
150 ml (5 fl oz) fish stock (see pages 15–16)
1 bay leaf
salt and freshly ground black pepper
450 g (1 lb) fish such as smoked haddock, salmon, cod or turbot, skinned, boned and cut into bite-sized cubes
115 g (4 oz) large prawns
2 hard-boiled eggs, quartered
900 g (2 lb) potatoes, cubed
45 g (1½ oz) unsalted butter
50 g (2 oz) plain flour
2 tbsp double cream
1 tbsp chopped fresh parsley
1 tbsp chopped fresh dill
115 g (4 oz) Cheddar cheese, grated
50 g (2 oz) white breadcrumbs

Method

- Put the milk, fish stock and bay leaf in a saucepan and season with salt and pepper. Add the fish and prawns and poach gently for 10 minutes. Lift the fish out carefully, using a slotted spoon, and place it in the bottom of an ovenproof pie dish.
- Place the quartered hard-boiled eggs among the pieces of fish in the bottom of the pie dish.
- Place the potatoes in a saucepan containing lightly salted boiling water and

cook for 15–20 minutes until they are soft. Drain the potatoes, add 15 g (½ oz) butter and 2 teaspoons of the cooking liquor from the fish and mash using a fork or potato masher until the potato is creamy and there are no lumps. Set aside.

- Preheat the oven to 220°C (425°F/Gas mark 7). Melt the remaining butter in a saucepan and then remove the pan from the heat. Add the flour and stir until it starts to come away from the side of the pan. Sieve the liquor the fish was cooked in and gradually add this to the roux in the saucepan, whisking continually to combine. Put the pan back on the heat and keep adding the liquor until you have a thick, creamy sauce, whisking constantly. Remove the pan from the heat and add the double cream and chopped herbs, stirring thoroughly to combine. Season with salt and pepper to taste.
- Pour the sauce over the top of the fish and hard-boiled eggs. Top with the mashed potato so that it completely covers the top and seal the edges by pressing a fork into the sides of the dish.
- Combine the grated cheese and the breadcrumbs and season with a little black pepper. Sprinkle over the top of the potato and then bake in the oven for 20 minutes or until the top is golden-brown.

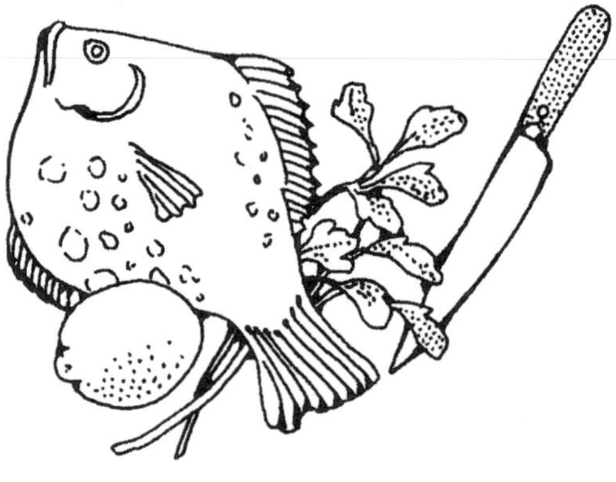

The Simplest Way to Fillet a Fish

Many recipes call for your fish to be filleted – that is, removed from the backbone. Although your local fishmonger will do this at your request, if you are lucky enough to have someone to catch some fresh fish for you, it is handy to know how to do it yourself. The secret is to have a really sharp filleting knife and a steel handy to resharpen it after each fish. Your first efforts may leave quite a lot of flesh behind, but with practice you will soon get the hang of it.

1. Start at the head end and find the fleshy point just behind the gill. Holding the head firmly, slice down into this soft spot at a slight angle towards the tail. Now turn the knife blade so that it is lying flat on top of the backbone.

2. Using a very slight sawing motion, slice the meat away from the backbone towards the tail. Do not slice the meat completely away from the tail – leave a small amount intact.

3. Next, flip the fish over, keeping the first fillet neatly underneath the body, and repeat steps 1 and 2.

4. When you have sliced both fillets from the backbone you can cut off the tail. At this point you should have two whole fillets with the skin left on one side.

5. To remove the skin from the fillets, hold the tail end with your fingers, slide a very sharp filleting knife between the skin and the flesh and gently work your way across the fillet until the skin is removed.

Homemade Cured Salmon

We always considered having smoked salmon for Sunday afternoon tea as a special treat, as it is quite expensive to buy. This is my version of cured salmon which, although it is not actually smoked, is even more delicious than anything you can buy in the shops. It is very easy to do, but you have to be a little patient while you wait for the salt and sugar to do their magic.

Serves 6–8

3 tbsp sea salt
3 tbsp caster sugar
1 tsp English mustard powder
1 tsp freshly ground black pepper
2 large handfuls of fresh dill, roughly chopped
900 g (2 lb) salmon fillet, skin and bones removed

Method

- In a small bowl, combine the salt, sugar, mustard powder and black pepper. Rub this mixture all over the salmon, making sure that you do not leave any of the flesh uncovered.
- Spread half the chopped dill in the base of a glass dish that is large enough to take the salmon fillet.
- Lay the salmon on top of the dill and put the remainder of the dill on top, covering the whole surface of the fish.
- Cover tightly with two layers of clingfilm and then find something you can lay on top to press down on the fish – ideally, a board of some kind that will fit inside the dish, weighed down with a couple of full tins that you have in your cupboard.
- Place the dish and its weights in the fridge and leave it for three days.
- At the end of the three days, remove the fish and wipe it down, using some damp kitchen paper to remove the dill and sugar/salt paste. Slice it very thinly using a sharp knife and serve as you would smoked salmon.

Smoked Haddock Kedgeree

Kedgeree is one of those meals that is suitable for any time of day. My grandfather used to love a plate piled high with this spicy food for breakfast and would eat up the leftovers at supper.

Serves 4

175 g (6 oz) long-grained rice
450 g (1 lb) smoked haddock
300 ml (10 fl oz) milk
salt and freshly ground black pepper
50 g (2 oz) unsalted butter
1 tsp mustard seeds
1 tsp cumin seeds
1 large onion, finely chopped
1 thumb-sized piece of fresh root ginger, grated
2 garlic cloves, finely chopped
4 tsp medium curry powder
1 red chilli, deseeded and finely sliced
200 ml (7 fl oz) chicken stock (see pages 11–12)
2 tbsp crème fraîche
3 hard-boiled eggs, chopped
fresh parsley, to garnish

Method

- Boil the rice according to the instructions on the packet and set aside.
- Poach the fish in seasoned milk for 10 minutes. Drain and flake the fish.
- Heat the butter in a large, deep frying pan on medium heat, add the mustard and cumin seeds and cook until you start to hear a popping sound. Add the onion, ginger and garlic and fry until the onion becomes translucent but not brown. Stir in the curry powder and chilli and continue to cook for another minute, stirring constantly.

- Add the flaked fish and cooked rice to the pan and pour the chicken stock over the top. Cook until the liquid starts to thicken up.
- Add the crème fraîche and cook for a further minute.
- Tip the kedgeree onto individual serving plates and top with the chopped egg and plenty of parsley.

Fish Cakes

This is probably one of the simplest recipes in this book, but simplicity does not mean that any of the flavours are sacrificed. This was always one of my favourite meals when I came home from school and I know the same thing can be said of my children and grandchildren, as they always ask me to make them when they come to stay. The coriander gives a slightly oriental flavour, but you can substitute fresh parsley if you prefer.

Serves 8

450 g (1 lb) white fish
300 ml (10 fl oz) milk
1 bay leaf
salt and freshly ground black pepper
4 medium potatoes, chopped
25 g (1 oz) unsalted butter
2 tbsp chopped fresh coriander
4 spring onions, chopped
1 large egg, beaten
115 g (4 oz) fresh breadcrumbs
75 g (2½ oz) parmesan cheese, grated
a little oil for frying

Method

- Place the fish in a saucepan together with the milk and bay leaf. Season with salt and pepper. Cook until the fish is tender and flaky. Drain, and,

once cool, flake with your fingers, removing any bones and skin. Set aside.
- Boil the potatoes in some lightly salted water until cooked through – about 15–20 minutes. Drain well and mash with the butter until the mixture is smooth and free of lumps.
- Stir the flaked fish, chopped coriander and spring onions into the potato mixture. Season well and mix thoroughly to combine all the ingredients.
- Put the beaten egg in one bowl and in a second bowl combine the breadcrumbs and grated parmesan.
- Form the potato and fish mixture into 8 thick fish cakes, using lightly floured hands. Dip each fish cake into the beaten egg and then roll gently in the breadcrumbs, pressing on them so that they are totally coated.
- Heat a little oil in a frying pan and cook the fish cakes over a medium heat until they are golden brown on both sides. Allow about 4 minutes each side to ensure they are warmed all the way through.

Prawn Cocktail

At one time, many a dinner party was graced with prawn cocktail as a first course. Although this 'posh' starter has gone out of fashion today, served with a wonderful homemade Marie Rose sauce it is a complement to any meal. It is very simple and quick to make and is a starter I most definitely recommend – you do not have to wait for a dinner party!

Serves 2 as a starter

250 g (9 oz) cooked, peeled prawns
1 Little Gem lettuce
2 slices of lemon, to garnish

For the Marie Rose sauce:

2 tbsp mayonnaise
1 tbsp tomato ketchup
1 tbsp double cream
1 tsp lemon juice
1 tsp smoked paprika
salt and freshly ground black pepper

Method

- ❖ Put all the ingredients for the Marie Rose sauce in a bowl and mix to combine thoroughly. Put a few prawns to one side to decorate the side of the glasses. Put the remainder of the prawns into the sauce and mix until they are all coated in the rosy pink sauce.
- ❖ Separate the leaves from the Little Gem lettuce, wash thoroughly and shred them.
- ❖ Place a layer of lettuce in the bottom of each glass, top with a heaped spoonful of the prawns and Marie Rose sauce and then decorate the edges of the glass with the reserved prawns. Sprinkle the top with a little extra paprika and serve chilled with a slice of lemon and some thin slices of brown bread and butter.

Potted Shrimp

Potted shrimp is not a dish you see very often on the menu these days, but it was very popular in my grandmother's day. It was traditionally made from tiny brown shrimp which were moulded into a small glass pot in seasoned butter and then turned out to eat with fresh bread or toast. If you want to add a little extra spice you can include ½ teaspoon of Tabasco sauce to the pan when cooking, but be careful you do not overdo it as it is very hot!

Serves 4

600 ml (1 pint) uncooked brown shrimp, peeled
salt and freshly ground black pepper to taste
150 g (5 oz) unsalted butter
1 garlic clove, crushed
1 tbsp finely chopped chives
½ tsp cayenne pepper
½ tsp nutmeg
½ tsp Worcestershire sauce
fresh watercress and lemon slices, to garnish

Method

- Season the shrimp with salt and pepper.
- Put the butter and crushed garlic clove in a small saucepan and allow the butter to melt gently. Leave to cook slowly until the garlic softens and infuses its flavour into the butter.
- Add the shrimp to the saucepan and stir to cover them thoroughly with the butter mixture.
- Add the rest of the ingredients to the pan and cook for a further 5 minutes, stirring continuously. Take care that you do not allow the mixture to boil at this stage.
- Fill individual ramekins with the shrimp mixture and press down lightly so they are packed tightly. Once cool, place the ramekins in the fridge and leave them until you are ready to serve.
- Serve with some fresh watercress, slices of lemon and some chunky slices of wholemeal bread or rolls.

Smoked Mackerel Pâté

Serves 6

350 g (12 oz) smoked mackerel fillets
1 lime
2 tsp prepared horseradish
150 g (5 oz) cream cheese
freshly ground black pepper
fresh watercress, to garnish

Method

- Remove the skin from the mackerel fillets and flake the flesh into the bowl of a food processor. Use your fingers to check there are no fine bones.
- Add the juice of half the lime, the prepared horseradish, the cream cheese, and about a teaspoon of freshly ground black pepper. Whizz until you have a smooth pâté.

- Check the seasoning and adjust as required, then place in a bowl and chill for several hours before serving.
- Serve on some thin slices of toast with some watercress and slices of lime.

Pâté Using Tuna

For a variation on the above recipe, whizz together the following ingredients in a blender for a smooth tuna pâté.

2 × 198 g (7 oz) cans tuna, drained
8 oz (225 g) creamed cheese
1 red chilli, deseeded and chopped
2 tbsp chopped fresh parsley
1 small onion, finely chopped
1 tsp Worcestershire sauce

Soused Herrings

This form of pickled herring is sometimes referred to as a rollmop and every time I prepare some for a treat it takes me right back to my childhood and the smell of my grandfather's pickling liquor. For some reason this was not a job my grandmother ever attempted, but the male tradition did not get handed down and in the succeeding generations it became my recipe. As an alternative you could use mackerel instead of herrings.

Serves 4

6 fresh herrings (about 200 g/7 oz each)
2 shallots, sliced into rings
6 black peppercorns

sprig of fresh thyme
2 bay leaves
1 tsp mustard seeds
2 tsp demerara sugar
sea salt
150 ml (5 fl oz) cider vinegar
150 ml (5 fl oz) water

Method

- Preheat the oven to 180°C (350°F/Gas mark 4).
- Start by scraping the scales from the herrings. Remove the heads and tails and then slit them down the belly to remove the roes. Wash the fish under cold running water and then lay them open on a board and run your thumb along the backbone. Turn them over and gently pull the bones away from the flesh, carefully picking out any stray bones with a pair of tweezers. Cut each fish into two fillets.
- Next, roll the fillets up from the head end and hold them in place using wooden cocktail sticks.
- Place each roll in the base of a shallow ovenproof dish. Add the shallots, peppercorns, herbs, mustard seeds and sugar and sprinkle generously with some sea salt. Pour the vinegar and water over the top and then cover the dish completely with a layer of kitchen foil.
- Stand the dish inside a deep baking tray containing about 5 cm (2 in) of boiling water. Place in the oven and bake for 30–35 minutes.
- Take out of the oven and leave the herrings to cool in their own liquor. They will keep for several days in the fridge and will taste even better after they have stood for a while as this gives the flavours time to penetrate the fish.

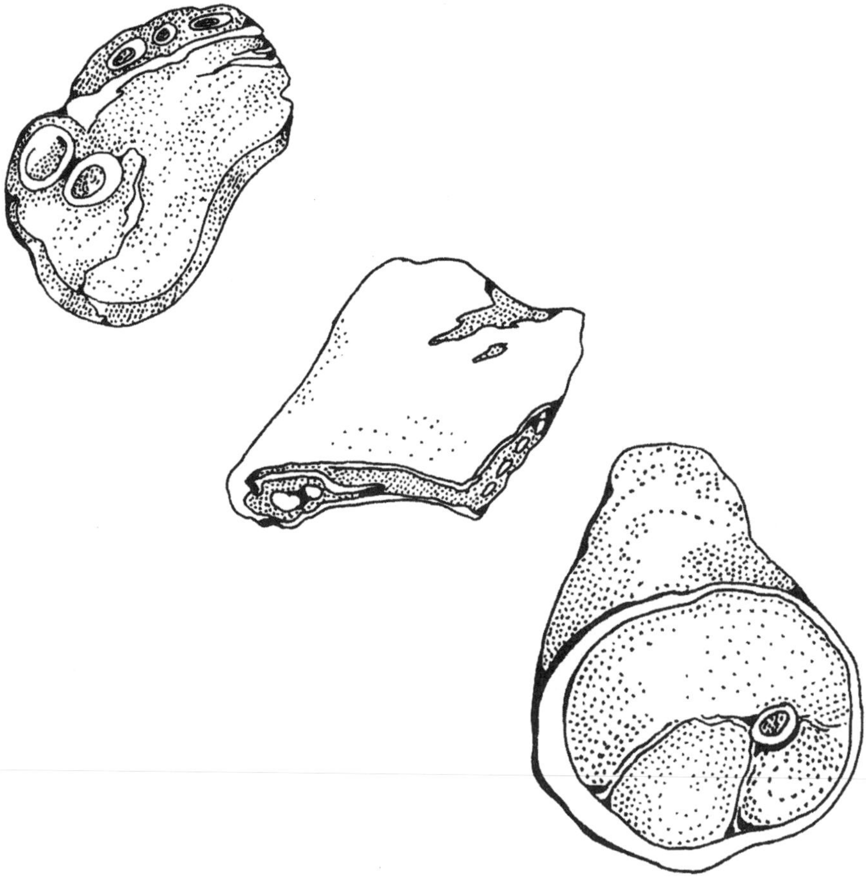

MEAT

Meat is probably one of the most versatile ingredients that a cook can use. It can be grilled, roasted, fried, barbecued, stewed or braised, according to the part of the animal from where it came, and the amount of cooking it requires to make it tender.

Cooking Meat

The recipes in this section use some of the cheaper joints of meat or the leftovers from a Sunday roast. Many people avoid the cheaper cuts, for example brisket or beef skirt, because they do not recognize the name and do not know what to do with them. Although they will require longer cooking than the more well-known cuts, you will not lose out on any of the flavour and you will save quite a few pennies as well. Hopefully some of my recipes will encourage you to give them a try, because you too can be like my grandmother's generation of home cooks, who were experts at making very little go a long way.

Unfortunately, as more and more butchers are being forced to close down because they cannot compete with the large supermarkets, consumers are being left with only the more expensive and well-known cuts of meat, as the choice is much smaller on the supermarket shelves. However, here are details of the wider range of beef, pork and lamb cuts – and of course the more you use a local butcher who can provide them, the more likely it is that they will remain available to you.

CUTS OF BEEF

Braising steak (also known as blade) does not require quite so much cooking as stewing steak (see below) and is suitable for use in casseroles, stews and any recipe that requires slow cooking.

Brisket is often sold salted, and generally the butcher will remove the bones and roll it for you. It works very well in pot roasts and slow-cooking casseroles.

Fillet (also referred to as tenderloin) is one of the finest cuts of beef as it is very tender and has very little fat. If you want to guarantee tenderness go for this cut, but remember it will be expensive. This is the traditional cut of beef used to make Beef Wellington.

Flank is usually sold as mince and is suitable for cottage pie, homemade beefburgers and spaghetti bolognese. However, if you see 'flash fry' steaks on a supermarket shelf, these are generally flank.

Fore rib is usually sold on the bone. It is excellent for a Sunday roast as it is tender and has a rich flavour.

Rump is a popular choice of beef, although it is not as tender as fillet or sirloin. It can be cooked quickly so is suitable for barbecuing, grilling or stir-frying.

Silverside is suitable for roasting as a joint, although you will need to remember to keep basting it to keep it moist. It requires a little longer cooking time than other roasting joints.

Sirloin is a tender cut of beef which is suitable to be eaten as either a steak or a roasting joint.

Stewing steak is one of the tougher cuts and is only suitable for recipes that require long, slow cooking.

Topside is ideal for roasting and often comes tied with a roll of fat to keep it moist during cooking. If not, regular basting will help to keep this cut of meat moist and tender.

CUTS OF PORK

Belly is the fatty area of the pig and therefore produces really tasty meat. Bacon is made from this cut of pork, but it is also suitable for roasting – although it does require slow cooking to become really tender. You can also cut it into strips and cook it on the barbecue for a tasty, crispy alternative to chops.

Chump is the area where chops and steaks are cut from. It is a reasonably priced cut of pork and is suitable for grilling or frying.

Hock is an economical cut which requires slow cooking but adds great flavour to stews, casseroles and soups as it is usually smoked.

Leg is the best joint for roasting, but is more expensive than many of the other cuts. It is also cured to make bacon, gammon joints and ham.

Loin is another roasting cut of pork and the area where bone-in chops come from. Bacon is also made from this cut and you can also buy it rolled and stuffed.

Neck end is often made into mince and is one of the cheaper cuts of pork. It is also cured for gammon joints which can either be roasted or boiled.

Pigs' trotters are the feet of the pig and they are gradually making a comeback after years of being ignored. They are best cooked slowly, preferably in a stock containing vegetables.
Ribs are a good choice for barbecuing or roasting and are relatively inexpensive.
Shoulder is a good choice for an economical roasting joint as it has a rich flavour and stays moist when cooked slowly. It is often used to make mince and sausages too.

CUTS OF LAMB
Foreshank is only really suitable for slow cooking, so works well in braised dishes, casseroles and stews.
Leg is the most popular choice of lamb for roasting, but is the most expensive to buy. If you do not want to go to the expense of a whole joint, it can be bought in leg steaks which are suitable for grilling or barbecuing.
Loin is the most tender cut of lamb and can be bought as steaks, small roasting joints and, for special occasions, lamb medallions. Loin can be roasted, grilled, fried or barbecued successfully.
Neck is usually sold as mince or stewing lamb as this is the tough area. The flavour is good, but it will require a lot of cooking in a liquid to keep it moist.
Rack is the most expensive cut to buy but makes a delicious roasting joint which is succulent and full of flavour.
Scrag end is another tough cut of lamb and is only suitable for stews and casseroles as it requires long, slow cooking.
Shoulder is another roasting joint, but is not so easy to carve as it contains a lot of bone. However, if you wish to spend a little more money you can have it boned and rolled.

Meatloaf

This is where my old mincer comes out of the cupboard and is put to use. Today you can buy prepared packs of just about any kind of mince – lamb, pork, beef or chicken – but I still prefer to make my own as that way I know exactly how much fat has gone into the final recipe. For my meatloaf I like to use a combination of both beef and pork, but if you prefer you can use just one or the other – remember to double the quantity. This is another extremely quick and easy recipe, which makes a delicious dish that can be served either hot or cold at any time of day.

Serves 4

unsalted butter for greasing
225 g (8 oz) minced beef
225 g (8 oz) minced pork
1 large onion, finely chopped
1 garlic clove, finely chopped
50 g (2 oz) white breadcrumbs
1 egg, lightly beaten
2 tbsp finely chopped fresh parsley
1 tsp finely chopped fresh sage
1 tsp finely chopped fresh thyme
1 tbsp Worcestershire sauce
salt and freshly ground black pepper
8 rashers of smoked streaky bacon

Method

- Preheat the oven to 190°C (375°F/Gas mark 5).
- Combine all the ingredients except the bacon in a large bowl, using your hands.
- Line a rectangular loaf tin with the rashers of bacon, allowing the strips to hang over the edge of the dish.

- Spoon the meat mixture into the middle of the dish, pressing it down firmly with the back of the spoon. Fold the edges of the bacon over the top of the meatloaf and press down firmly.
- Bake in the centre of the oven for 45–50 minutes. Remove from the oven and allow to cool before slicing.

Cottage Pie / Shepherd's Pie

This potato-topped dish has traditionally been made to use up leftover meat. The recipe is the same for both pies with the exception of the meat – minced beef for the Cottage Pie and minced lamb for the Shepherd's Pie.

Serves 4

1 kg (2¼ lb) large, floury potatoes, diced
salt and freshly ground black pepper
50 g (2 oz) unsalted butter
a splash of milk
1 large onion, diced
1 carrot, diced
1 celery stick, diced
525 g (1 lb 3 oz) minced beef or lamb
1 tbsp chopped fresh thyme
1 tbsp chopped fresh parsley
½ tsp ground cinnamon
1 tbsp tomato purée
a few shakes of Worcestershire sauce
350 ml (12 fl oz) beef or vegetable stock (see pages 12–13 and 14–15)
115 g (4 oz) Cheddar cheese, grated

Method

- Boil the potatoes in lightly salted water until they are soft. Drain thoroughly and then mash, adding half the butter and a splash of milk, until they are of a creamy consistency. Set aside.

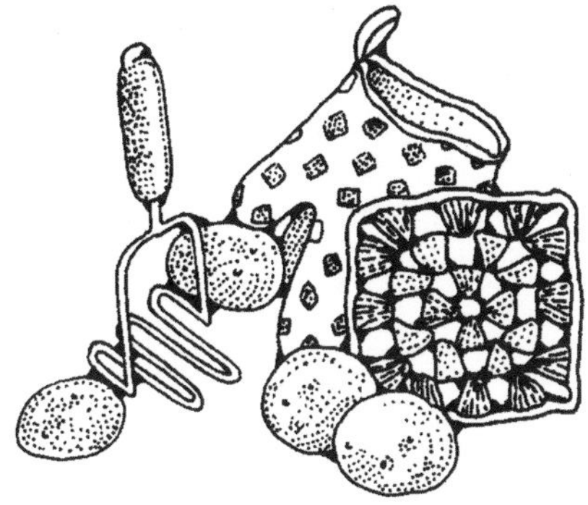

- Preheat the oven to 200°C (400°F/Gas mark 6).
- Heat the remaining butter in a large frying pan. When it has melted add the chopped onion, carrot and celery and cook until the onion starts to go brown. Add the minced meat and cook until it has browned thoroughly.
- Add the herbs, cinnamon, tomato purée, Worcestershire sauce and stock. Allow the mixture to simmer gently for about 30 minutes, uncovered, until the stock starts to thicken.
- Tip the mixture into an ovenproof dish and then cover with a thick layer of mashed potato, making sure you seal the edges with a fork. Run the fork over the top of the potato to make furrows as this will help it to crisp up in the oven.
- Cover the top of the potato with a layer of grated cheese and a few extra dots of butter.
- Place in the preheated oven and bake for around 40 minutes, or until the top is brown and crispy.

Grandmother's Variations

- Instead of carrots and celery, use some leeks and turnips to give it a slightly different flavour.
- The mashed potato can be replaced with mashed sweet potato or mashed butternut squash and browned in the oven in exactly the same way.

Braised Shin of Beef

To get the best out of a shin of beef it requires long, slow cooking and this recipe really brings out the intense flavour of the meat. It is all cooked in one pot in the oven.

Serves 4–6

1 tbsp flour
salt and freshly ground pepper
1 kg/2¼ lb shin of beef, trimmed of fat and cut into 2.5 cm (1 in) cubes
3 tbsp olive oil
3 garlic cloves, left whole
1 large onion, roughly chopped
2 celery sticks, diced
2 carrots, diced
1 parsnip, diced
150 ml (5 fl oz) beef stock (see pages 12–13)
100 ml (3½ fl oz) red wine
400 g (14 oz) can plum tomatoes
1 tsp smoked hot paprika
1 bouquet garni
sprig of fresh rosemary
12 button mushrooms, whole

Method

- Preheat the oven to 180°C (350°F/Gas mark 4).
- Put the flour in a freezer bag and season with salt and pepper. Add the meat to the bag, hold the top firmly and shake until all the meat has a coating of flour.
- Heat 1 tablespoon olive oil in a large frying pan and then brown the meat in batches, making sure you do not overcrowd the pan. Place the browned meat in a large ovenproof casserole.

- Add more oil to the frying pan and cook the garlic, onion, celery, carrots and parsnip until they start to go brown. Once browned, add them to the casserole dish with the meat.
- Now add the stock, wine, tomatoes, paprika and a little salt and pepper to the frying pan and stir well to make sure you incorporate all the residue from frying the meat and the vegetables. Allow the stock to come to the boil and then simmer for a further 10 minutes.
- Transfer the contents of the frying pan to the casserole, then add the bouquet garni, rosemary and mushrooms and cover with a tight-fitting lid. If the lid does not fit tightly, put a double layer of kitchen foil beneath it.
- Cook in the oven for at least 3 hours, or until the meat is tender and breaks apart easily. Check the seasoning, remove the bouquet garni and rosemary and serve with a large helping of mashed potato.

Beef Stew with Herby Dumplings

The art of stewing meat has been around for aeons, and because the cooking is done slowly you can use cheaper cuts. The secret of a great stew is not to rush it – the longer you cook it the better it will taste. In fact, Grandmother always said that a stew tasted better on the second day because the flavours had had more time to combine. This was definitely one of Grandmother's winter warmers and one that I still serve up to my family on a regular basis. After an afternoon of sledging or having snowball fights, as children we sat round the old trestle table in Grandmother's kitchen and tucked into this stew which quickly warmed our chilly fingers and toes.

Serves 4

900 g (2 lb) chuck steak, trimmed of fat and cut into cubes
2 tbsp plain flour, seasoned
1 tsp fresh thyme leaves
25 g (1 oz) lard
2 medium onions, diced
2 carrots, sliced
2 celery sticks, sliced
225 g (8 oz) button mushrooms
1 tsp English mustard powder
360 ml (12 fl oz) brown ale or stout
1 bouquet garni
salt and freshly ground black pepper

For the Herby Dumplings:
115 g (4 oz) self-raising flour
½ tsp salt
50 g (2 oz) suet (vegetarian suet works just as well)
1 tsp fresh thyme, finely chopped
1 tsp fresh oregano, finely chopped
1 tsp fresh chives, finely chopped

Method

- Coat the cubes of beef in a mixture of seasoned flour and thyme by placing them in a large freezer bag and shaking until the meat is completely coated.
- Heat the lard in a large frying pan and add the beef. Sauté until it is browned on all sides, then add the onions and cook for 3 minutes.
- Tip the meat and onion mixture into a large, heavy-based saucepan. Add the remaining vegetables and the mustard powder and then pour in the brown ale or stout. Add the bouquet garni, season lightly with salt and pepper and then bring to the boil. Reduce the heat to low and cook for at least 2 hours, checking and stirring every 30 minutes to make sure that the stew is not sticking to the bottom of the pan. If the gravy is too thick, stir in a little water.
- While the stew is cooking, make the dumplings. Sieve the flour with

the salt in a bowl and add the suet and chopped herbs. Mix together thoroughly and then make a small well in the middle. Add enough cold water to make a stiff dough. Flour your hands and work the dough into little balls (about the size of a golf ball).

- Fifteen minutes before the end of the cooking time, check that the meat is really tender, add the dumplings and cook for a further 15 minutes. Check the seasoning and serve.

Tripe and Onions

Tripe is the stomach lining of a cow and is one of those animal parts that fell from favour but is now making a reappearance, served by adventurous chefs. Cooked in this way it makes an economical, filling and delicious meal which is very easy for anyone with a delicate stomach to digest. You will probably not find tripe in your local supermarket, but your butcher should have it.

Serves 4

450 g (1 lb) trimmed tripe
3 onions, sliced
600 ml (1 pint) milk
100 ml (3½ fl oz) crème fraîche
1 tsp grated nutmeg
2 bay leaves
salt and freshly ground black pepper
25 g (1 oz) unsalted butter
3 tbsp plain flour
chopped fresh parsley, to garnish

Method

- Place the tripe in a saucepan and cover it with cold water. Bring to the boil, then drain and rinse under cold running water. This will help to soften it. Cut the tripe into small pieces of equal size, so that they all cook evenly.

- Put the prepared tripe in a large saucepan with the onions, milk, crème fraîche, nutmeg, bay leaves, salt and pepper and bring to the boil. Put the lid on the saucepan, turn the heat down and simmer for 2½–3 hours or until the tripe is really tender.
- At the end of the cooking period, drain the tripe, reserving 600 ml (1 pint) of the liquid.
- Melt the butter in a saucepan, add the flour and cook over a gentle heat for 1½–2 minutes, stirring all the time. Remove the pan from the heat and stir in the reserved cooking liquor a little at a time. Return to the heat and keep stirring until the sauce thickens.
- Add the tripe and onions to the sauce, adjust the seasoning and reheat. Garnish with chopped parsley and serve with new potatoes.

Faggots with Onion Gravy

Faggots are balls of minced meat that were traditionally made from offcuts or cheaper cuts and then cooked in the oven rather than fried. They have rather gone out of favour in today's culinary world, but they are a delicious alternative to regular meatballs. If you do not have a mincer or a food processor to chop the meat very finely, your butcher may be prepared to mince everything for you.

Serves 6

450 g (1 lb) lean beef, minced
115 g (4 oz) lamb's liver, minced
115 g (4 oz) streaky bacon, minced
1 onion, finely chopped
2 garlic cloves, finely chopped
50 g (2 oz) fresh white breadcrumbs
1 tbsp chopped fresh parsley
1 tbsp chopped fresh sage
1 tbsp chopped fresh thyme

2 tsp Dijon mustard
salt and freshly ground black pepper
1 egg, beaten

For the onion gravy:
25 g (1 oz) unsalted butter
2 large onions, finely chopped
1 tbsp plain flour
600 ml (1 pint) hot beef stock (see pages 12–13)
300 ml (10 fl oz) ale or stout
few drops of Worcestershire sauce
salt and freshly ground black pepper

Method

- Preheat the oven to 180°C (350°F/Gas mark 4).
- Put all the ingredients for the faggots in a large bowl. Using your hands, thoroughly combine them and then make 12 golf-ball size faggots.
- Now make your onion gravy by melting the butter in a large saucepan. Add the chopped onions and cook over a medium heat for about 5 minutes or until the onions are translucent. Add the flour and cook for a further 2–3 minutes, stirring constantly. Gradually add the hot beef stock, ale or stout, Worcestershire sauce and seasoning. Bring to the boil, reduce the heat and then simmer for about 5 minutes or until the gravy has thickened.
- Put the faggots in a deep ovenproof dish and pour the gravy over them. Cover the dish with a lid or kitchen foil and cook in the preheated oven for 1½–2 hours. Remove the lid or foil for the last 20 minutes, then serve. Creamy mashed potatoes are an excellent accompaniment.

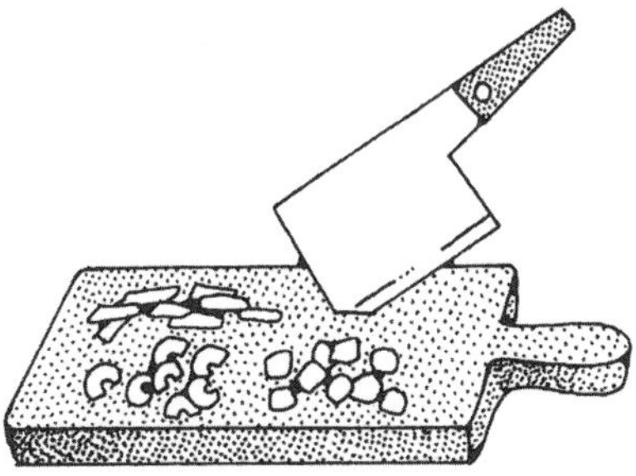

Layered Mutton and Potato Hotpot

Mutton is meat from a mature sheep and requires longer cooking than lamb. It has a more complex flavour than lamb and makes a scrumptious stew or, in this case, a hotpot. You may not be able to find mutton in a supermarket, but you should not have any trouble if you ask your local butcher.

Serves 4

2 tbsp plain flour
salt and freshly ground black pepper
450 g (1 lb) mutton, trimmed of fat and cut into 2.5 cm (1 in) cubes
50 g (2 oz) unsalted butter
3 onions, roughly chopped
3 garlic cloves, sliced
3 sprigs of fresh rosemary
5 sprigs of fresh thyme
3 carrots, cut into large chunks
1 turnip, cut into large chunks
2 celery sticks, cut into chunks
1 tbsp tomato purée
1 litre (1¾ pints) chicken stock (see pages 11–12)
6 potatoes, thinly sliced

Method

- Put the flour in a freezer bag and season with salt and pepper. Add the meat to the bag, hold the top firmly and shake until all the meat has a coating of flour.
- Melt 25 g (1 oz) butter in a large, heavy-based saucepan and add the meat. Cook until it browns, turning it regularly to make sure it is browned on all sides. Do not overcrowd the pan – brown the meat in batches if there is too much to make a single layer.

- Next, add the onions, garlic, rosemary and thyme to the saucepan and cook until the onions are soft and lightly browned.
- Add 25 g (1 oz) butter and the carrots, turnip and celery and cook for about 3 minutes, stirring frequently.
- Add the tomato purée and chicken stock and bring to the boil. Lower the heat to simmering point and then cover with the lid and cook for 30 minutes. Adjust the seasoning to your taste.
- Preheat the oven to 220°C (425°F/Gas mark 7).
- Take an ovenproof casserole dish with a lid and place a layer of potato in it, followed by a layer of mutton stew. Then make another layer of potatoes and stew and continue in this way until you have used up all the ingredients. Finish with a layer of potatoes, making sure that they overlap one another. Brush the top layer with a little of the meat gravy and cook in the oven for 30 minutes. Turn the oven down to 140°C (275°F/Gas mark 1) and leave to cook for a further 2 hours. This will ensure that the mutton is really tender.
- At the end of the cooking time turn the oven back up to 220°C (425°F/Gas mark 7. Remove the lid from the casserole dish and brush the top of the potatoes with the remaining butter, melted, to allow the potatoes to brown for the last 15 minutes.
- Serve this dish while it is piping hot, accompanied by a variety of seasonal vegetables.

Mutton Stew with Vegetables

This stew has so much flavour it is one that you will want to make time and time again. It is packed with vegetables so you really do not need to serve anything else with it – it is an economical one-pot meal which is great if you don't like washing up lots of pans. If you have difficulty finding mutton, simply substitute one of the cheaper cuts of lamb and cut down on the cooking time by about 15 minutes.

Serves 4–6

1 tbsp plain flour
600 g (1 lb 5 oz) mutton (either breast or neck), cut into 2.5 cm (1 in) cubes, with any excess fat removed
salt and freshly ground black pepper
50 g (2 oz) unsalted butter or lard
2 garlic cloves, chopped
1 large red onion, diced
2 celery sticks, diced
1 litre (1¾ pints) chicken stock (see pages 11–12)
1 tbsp fresh thyme, chopped
2 tbsp tomato purée
1 tsp English mustard powder
1 red chilli, deseeded and finely chopped
1 large potato, diced
2 medium carrots, diced
1 parsnip, diced

Method

- Put the flour in a plastic freezer bag and season with salt and pepper. Put the meat inside the bag, hold the top firmly and shake until all the meat has a coating of flour.
- Heat the butter or lard in a large casserole dish, making sure it is big enough to hold all the ingredients. When the butter or lard is melted and hot, brown the mutton in batches so there is room to turn it and brown it on all sides. Once all the meat is browned, return it to the casserole and add the garlic, onion and celery. Continue to cook for another 5 minutes or until the onion is starting to turn brown.
- Add the stock, thyme, tomato purée, mustard powder and chopped chilli and bring to the boil. Reduce the heat, put the lid on the casserole dish and allow the stew to simmer for 1½ hours.
- When the time is up, add the potato, carrots and parsnips and stir to combine all the ingredients. Bring the stew back to the boil and then reduce the heat and allow it to simmer for a further 40 minutes.

❖ Check the seasoning and add some additional salt and pepper if necessary. Serve the stew piping hot.

Pork with Apple Casserole

Direct from the pages of my grandmother's handwritten recipe book, this is a great dish to make in the autumn when the windfalls are lying at the bottom of the apple tree just waiting to be used. Pork loin is not the cheapest cut but it is wonderfully tender. However, if you want a more economical version of this recipe substitute pork shoulder and add an extra 20 minutes to the overall cooking time.

Serves 4

25 g (1 oz) butter
550 g (1¼ lb) pork loin or shoulder, trimmed of fat and cut into cubes
salt and freshly ground black pepper
1 onion, chopped
1 leek, sliced
12 shallots, whole
grated zest of ½ lemon
250 ml (8 fl oz) dry cider
200 ml (7 fl oz) chicken stock (see pages 11–12)
sprig of fresh thyme
4 sage leaves
2 apples (Granny Smiths work well in this recipe), peeled, cored and sliced
125 ml (4 fl oz) double cream
2 tbsp fresh parsley, finely chopped

Method

❖ Heat the butter in a large frying pan and brown the pork in batches, making sure not to overcrowd the pan. Stir frequently until the meat is nicely browned on all sides.

- Transfer the meat to a large, heavy-based pan.
- Return the frying pan to the heat and add the onion and leek. Brown gently for a few minutes, then add the lemon zest, cider, chicken stock, thyme and sage. Boil for about 5 minutes to let the flavours infuse.
- Pour the contents of the frying pan into the saucepan containing the pork and cook for 30 minutes or until the pork is tender.
- Next, add the sliced apples to the pan and cook for another 10 minutes or until the apple has softened but not broken up.

- Take the saucepan off the heat and, using a slotted spoon, remove the pork, onion, leek and apple to a warmed serving dish. Cover the dish and keep warm while you prepare the gravy.
- Add the double cream to the liquid left in the saucepan and allow the sauce to bubble gently until it starts to thicken. Stir in the parsley, check the seasoning and then pour over the top of the pork mixture in the serving dish. My favourite accompaniment to this dish is a large jacket potato, split open and with the pork casserole generously spooned on top.

Toad in the Hole

This is a recipe that dates back to the 18th century and consists of sausages lying in a Yorkshire pudding shell. Grandmother always served this with a rich onion gravy and a few peas tipped in the middle for good measure. The secret of a crispy pudding that rises properly is to have your fat smoking hot before putting the batter into the tin. You can either use lard, or if you want a healthier option use some vegetable oil as suggested in this recipe.

Serves 4

115 g (4 oz) plain flour
salt and freshly ground black pepper
2 eggs
300 ml (10 fl oz) milk
8 pork sausages
4 tbsp vegetable oil

Method

- Preheat the oven to 230°C (450°F/Gas mark 8).
- To make your Yorkshire pudding mix, place the flour and a pinch of salt in a bowl and make a well in the middle. Break the eggs into the well and gradually add the milk while mixing with a whisk. Keep whisking until you have added all the milk and you have a smooth, creamy batter with little air bubbles on the surface. Leave the batter to rest for 15 minutes and then whisk again just before you use it.
- While the batter is resting, heat 1 tablespoon oil in a frying pan and fry the sausages until they are lightly coloured – not too brown, as the oven will finish the cooking. Lift the sausages out of the pan and drain them on kitchen paper.
- Pour the fat in the frying pan into a small roasting tin, adding a little extra oil if necessary – there should be about 4 tablespoons in the bottom of the tin. Put the tin in the oven and allow it to heat up until the oil is smoking.
- Pour the batter into the hot tin and then gently lay the sausages in the centre. Immediately place the tin in the hot oven and bake for about 10 minutes.
- Reduce the heat to 200°C (400°F/Gas mark 6) and bake for a further 20 minutes or until the batter has risen and is a lovely golden colour.
- Make sure you have everyone sitting down at the table before you are ready to serve, because as soon as the pudding hits the colder air it will start to deflate! For the rich onion gravy that my grandmother served with this dish, see Faggots with Onion Gravy on pages 98–99.

Honey and Mustard Roasted Gammon

Gammon is ham that has been cured in the same way as bacon. You can buy a gammon joint either smoked or unsmoked, and this recipe works just as well with either. Gammon can be salty, so it is worth soaking it in cold water overnight before cooking.

Serves 4

2 kg (4½ lb) gammon joint
2 tbsp runny honey
1 tbsp wholegrain mustard
2 tsp Worcestershire sauce
1 tbsp balsamic vinegar
1 tbsp soft brown sugar
12 whole black peppercorns

Method

- Having already soaked the meat, drain it and put in a pan with some clean cold water. Bring to the boil, then turn down the heat and simmer with the lid on for 1 hour.
- While the gammon is cooking, put the honey, mustard, Worcestershire sauce, vinegar and sugar in a bowl and mix well.
- When the hour is up, preheat the oven to 200°C (400°F/Gas mark 6). Drain the gammon joint and then place it in a roasting tin. When it is cool enough to handle, remove the outer skin but leave some of the fat behind as this will go crispy when the joint is roasted. Stud the fat with the peppercorns and then pour the glaze over the surface, making sure that the whole joint is covered. Place the gammon in the oven and roast for another hour. Keep basting during the cooking time, checking that the top is not burning. If it is cooking too quickly, turn the heat down a little.
- Allow the joint to stand for 20 minutes before carving. This can be served either hot or cold and as an alternative meat for Sunday roast, perhaps accompanied by Spicy Caramelized Pineapple (see opposite).

Spicy Caramelized Pineapple

Pineapple makes a wonderful accompaniment to gammon and this spicy variation works really well with the roasted gammon recipe opposite. You will need some fresh pineapple rings, 1 tablespoon soft brown sugar, 25 g (1 oz) unsalted butter, 1 teaspoon wholegrain mustard and 1 teaspoon cayenne pepper. Simply melt the sugar and butter in a frying pan, stir in the mustard and then add the pineapple rings in single layers. Fry for about 2 minutes on each side or until they are browned and caramelized. Before serving sprinkle each slice with cayenne pepper to give that little extra kick!

STEAMED BACON PUDDING

This was one of my favourite meals as a child and Grandmother always served it piping hot with a dollop of pease pudding (see pages 45–46). It is very quick and easy to prepare, but you need to plan this meal in advance as it requires three hours of steaming for all the flavours to mingle.

Serves 4

225 g (8 oz) plain flour
½ tsp baking powder
½ tsp salt
115 g (4 oz) shredded suet
8 rashers of smoky bacon, de-rinded and finely chopped
2 onions, finely chopped
handful of sage leaves, finely chopped
freshly ground black pepper

Method

- To keep your suet pastry light, first sift the flour, baking powder and salt into a bowl. Add the suet and then, using your hands, gradually introduce cold water and knead until you have a soft dough.
- Place the dough onto a floured board and then, using a floured rolling pin, roll it out until you have an oblong shape.
- Mix the bacon with the chopped onion and then spread the mixture over the top of the pastry, leaving about 2.5 cm (1 in) all around the edge.
- Sprinkle the sage over the top of the bacon and onion mixture. Finally, season with freshly ground black pepper. You should not need any extra salt as the bacon should be salty enough.
- Dampen the edges of the suet dough with water and then roll up like a Swiss roll.
- Tie the pudding in a steaming cloth or cover the top with a piece of kitchen foil that has a fold in the middle and secure with string. Either place the pudding in the top of a steamer or stand it on an upturned saucer in a deep saucepan and then fill the saucepan three-quarters full with boiling water. Put on a medium heat and allow the pudding to steam for 3 hours.

Rabbit Casserole

Today, it is rare to see a whole rabbit hanging in a butcher's window as many modern cooks would find this distasteful, but it is still possible to buy rabbit joints that have been prepared if you are a little on the squeamish side. This casserole is rich and delicious and when served with a mound of creamy mashed potato will satisfy any hungry family.

Serves 4

50 g (1¾ oz) plain flour
salt and freshly ground black pepper
1 rabbit, cut into pieces
1 large onion, roughly chopped

2 garlic cloves, sliced
sprig of fresh rosemary
sprig of fresh thyme
25 g (1 oz) butter
600 ml (1 pint) chicken stock (see pages 11–12)
3 carrots, cut into chunks
2 potatoes, cut into chunks
1 turnip, cut into chunks
1 leek, sliced

Method

- Preheat the oven to 180°C (350°F/Gas mark 4). Put the flour in a plastic freezer bag and season with salt and pepper. Put the rabbit pieces inside the bag, hold the top firmly and shake until all they all have a coating of flour.
- Take a large casserole dish with a lid and spread the chopped onion and garlic over the bottom. Crush the rosemary and thyme sprigs to release their aroma and sprinkle them over the top of the onion mixture.
- In a large frying pan, heat the butter and lightly brown the floured rabbit pieces on all sides, turning frequently.
- Place the rabbit in the casserole dish on top of the onion mixture.
- Return the frying pan to the heat and add the chicken stock. Bring to the boil and then allow to simmer for 5 minutes to make sure all the sediment from the bottom of the pan is incorporated.
- Pour the stock over the rabbit and onion in the casserole dish and cover tightly with the lid. Place the casserole in the oven for 2½–3 hours or until the rabbit is tender and starting to fall off the bone.
- Remove the casserole from the oven and discard any bones that have lost their meat. Add the vegetables and return to the oven for another 45 minutes. If the casserole looks a little dry, add some more stock.
- This casserole can either be served as it is, or if you prefer a thicker gravy you can spoon some of the liquid into a saucepan and thicken it using some cornflour. Return the gravy to the casserole and cook for a further 10 minutes.

POULTRY

Nothing needs to be wasted when you are cooking poultry, as the bones can be boiled to make a delicious soup or stock and the leftover meat from a Sunday roast can be turned into a delicious curry or chicken and ham pie, for example.

Cooking Poultry

Grandfather always kept chickens and ducks in a large run at the bottom of the garden. Not only did they provide us with a constant supply of fresh eggs, but wonderfully tender and tasty meat as well. If you usually buy inexpensive prepackaged poultry from a supermarket, you may have found that you have to add plenty of herbs and seasoning to get a decent flavour. However, if you are prepared to pay extra for fresh farm poultry you will be amazed at the difference in flavour and the quality of the meat. When buying poultry from a butcher, do not be afraid to ask him where he sources his meat just to make sure that it is completely free range.

Many people are wary of handling raw chicken because of the possibility of salmonella poisoning. Although chicken does carry a certain risk of this bacteria, if you take some basic precautions it should not pose a health hazard. Here are a few simple steps to follow:

- When you go shopping, make sure that you keep raw chicken away from the rest of your produce so that blood does not drip on to other food items and contaminate them.

- Put your chicken in the fridge as soon as you get home, as salmonella bacteria cannot grow in cold temperatures.

- Make sure that frozen chicken is thoroughly thawed before cooking. This can be done by leaving it in the fridge overnight, putting it in a bowl of cold water for a few hours or defrosting it in a microwave. Remember, once your meat has thawed it cannot be refrozen unless you have cooked it first.

- After handling raw chicken, wash your hands thoroughly with hot water and soap. This also applies to any knives, cutting boards, dishes or any other utensils that have come into contact with the meat.

- Check that chicken is cooked thoroughly before serving. Small pieces can be cut in half to check that the middle is not still pink. If you are roasting a whole bird, insert a knife into the thickest part – the meat juices should run clear. If they are still pink, cook for a little longer and test again.

- Never leave cooked chicken standing at room temperature – put it in the fridge as soon as you can then it can be used safely on another day.

Perfect Roast Chicken

The aroma of a chicken roasting in the oven is enough to make anyone's mouth water. I always start with the chicken upside down so that the juices run into the breast and then turn it the right way up for the last 30 minutes to crisp the skin. You can choose whatever you like to stuff the cavity, but a whole lemon is simple and give a zesty flavour to the flesh. I also add onions and celery in the base of the dish, which contributes to a really tasty gravy.

Serves 4

1 medium-sized chicken (about 1.8 kg/4 lb in weight)
25 g (1 oz) unsalted butter
salt and freshly ground black pepper
1 lemon
few sprigs of fresh thyme, rosemary or sage (or all three)
2 onions, unpeeled, cut into quarters
2 garlic cloves, unpeeled, crushed
2 celery sticks
1 tbsp plain flour

Method

- Preheat the oven to 220°C (425°F/Gas mark 7). Remove any giblets from the chicken and wash it inside and out. Pat dry with some kitchen paper.

Next rub the skin with the butter and then season thoroughly with salt and freshly ground black pepper.

- Carefully pierce the skin of the lemon in several places and then place it inside the cavity of the chicken, together with the fresh herbs.
- Put the chicken upside down in a deep roasting tin and surround it with the onion quarters, crushed garlic and celery; the onion and garlic skins will help to colour the gravy. Pour some hot water into the roasting tin and place it in the oven for 1 hour. Then remove the roasting tin from the oven, turn the chicken the right side up, baste it with the juices and return to the oven for another 30 minutes or until the juices run clear.
- Transfer the chicken to a board to rest while you make the gravy.
- Mix the flour with a little of the juice from the roasting tin until you have a smooth mixture with no lumps. Slowly add this to the roasting juices and then cook on top of the stove for 3–4 minutes, or until the gravy has thickened. Strain the gravy through a fine sieve and serve in a gravy boat so that people can take as much as they like.

The Easiest Way to Carve a Chicken

- Allow the chicken to stand for at least 15 minutes before attempting to carve. Using a really sharp knife, carefully cut down between the breast of the bird and its legs. Use a slight seesaw motion to cut through the joint and then pull the leg away from the bird on both sides. Cut the leg in half so that you have both a thigh and a drumstick and place them on the outside of the serving plate.
- Remove the breast by placing your knife at the same angle as the breastbone and gently cutting away the meat on both sides. You can either leave this whole or carve it into slices once you have removed it.
- The fiddly bits that are left on the bones are most easily removed with your fingers. Make sure you get all the tasty bits from the underside of the bird.
- Do not throw the carcass away – use it to make soup or stock for another recipe.

Grandmother's Chicken Stew

I don't know about you, but I think there is something particularly comforting about a traditional chicken stew. The smell that permeates my kitchen every time I cook this recipe takes me right back to my days with my own grandmother, who always served her stew in a large bowl with a piece of homemade soda bread. There are a lot of ingredients in this recipe, but it really is worth the effort and tastes even better when heated up on the second day. Traditionally, this recipe would have been made with a whole chicken, but to make it quicker I suggest that you use chicken breasts instead.

Serves 4

450 g (1 lb) skinless chicken breasts, cut into bite-sized chunks
salt and freshly ground black pepper
25 g (1 oz) butter
2 garlic cloves, sliced
1 large onion, chopped
225 g (8 oz) button mushrooms, whole
1 leek, sliced
600 ml (1 pint) chicken stock (see pages 11–12)
sprig of fresh marjoram
sprig of fresh thyme
2 bay leaves
2 potatoes, cubed
1 parsnip, sliced
2 carrots, sliced
1 sweet potato, cubed
1 tsp sweet paprika
1 tbsp cornflour
125 ml (4 fl oz) sour cream

Method

❖ Season the chicken well with salt and pepper.

- Heat the butter in a large frying pan and then add the seasoned chicken pieces. Brown on all sides and then remove and place them in a large saucepan.
- Return the frying pan to the heat and add the garlic, onion, mushrooms and leek. Cook gently for 5 minutes or until the onion has become translucent. Add the chicken stock to the pan along with the herbs and bring to the boil. Turn the heat down and simmer for 5 minutes to allow all the flavours to infuse.
- Put the remaining vegetables in the saucepan containing the chicken and add the sweet paprika. Pour the stock over the vegetables. Bring the stock back to the boil, reduce the heat, cover the saucepan and simmer for 30 minutes.
- Mix the cornflour with a little cold water and a few tablespoons of the hot gravy from the chicken stew. Slowly pour this back into the stew, making sure you keep stirring to prevent it from going lumpy. This is to thicken the stew and to help make the flavours more intense.
- Remove the bay leaves and stir in the sour cream. Check the seasoning and adjust as necessary. Heat gently and then serve piping hot with some new potatoes.

Chicken and Leek Pie

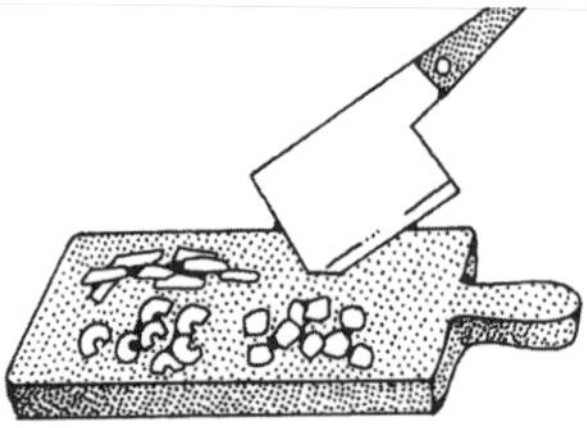

Pies, both sweet and savoury, are among my favourite meals. This one has a wonderful light puff pastry and a creamy filling of leek and chicken. I have always made my own pastry, following in my grandmother's footsteps, but if you are busy you can cheat and buy the readymade pastry to be found on the chilled counter at the supermarket. Some people like to have a pastry base and others just a topping; I find a good thick layer of puff pastry on top of the pie is quite enough and you do not risk ending up with a soggy base.

Serves 4–6

3 chicken legs
salt and freshly ground black pepper
1 tsp olive oil
50 g (2 oz) butter
1 onion, finely diced
1 leek, thinly sliced
1 tbsp plain flour
1 tsp English mustard powder
1 tsp paprika
250 ml (8 fl oz) chicken stock (see pages 11–12)
120 ml (4 fl oz) milk
60 ml (2 fl oz) single cream
2 tbsp finely chopped fresh tarragon
50 g (2 oz) parmesan cheese, grated
1 sheet rough puff pastry (see pages 130–131)
1 egg, beaten, for glazing

Method

- Preheat the oven to 200°C (400°F/Gas mark 6). Season the chicken legs, drizzle with the olive oil and roast for 40 minutes or until the juices run clear. Wait for them to cool and then remove all the meat from the bone and cut into even-sized pieces. Set aside and reserve the cooking juices from the chicken as these will add extra flavour to the filling.
- To prepare the filling for the pie, melt the butter in a large frying pan or saucepan over a medium heat. Add the onion and leek and fry for about 5 minutes or until the onion is translucent and the leek is tender.
- Stir in the flour, mustard and paprika and cook over a low heat for about 2 minutes, stirring all the time so that it does not stick to the bottom of the pan. Gradually add the chicken stock and milk and the reserved juices from the cooked chicken, stirring constantly to avoid it becoming lumpy. Then stir in the cream and simmer for about 5 minutes or until the sauce starts to thicken.
- Once the sauce has thickened, add the chicken, tarragon, parmesan and

enough salt and pepper until you have the seasoning just right. Pour the filling into an ovenproof pie dish and leave to cool before putting on the pastry lid. If you put the lid on top of the filling while it is still hot, the pastry will not rise properly and will be soggy underneath.

- Preheat the oven to 190°C (375°F/Gas mark 5). Make your pastry according to the instructions on pages 130–131 and then roll it out until you have a sheet slightly larger than the circumference of your pie dish. Wet the edges of the pie dish with some water and then cut a couple of 1 cm (½ in) strips of pastry and lay them around the edges, pressing them down firmly with your fingers.
- Roll the remaining sheet of pastry around your rolling pin, then pick it up and lay it on one side of the pie dish. Gently unroll until it covers the whole surface. Press down on the edges with a fork to seal and then cut a couple of slits in the top to allow the steam to escape. Cut off any excess pastry from the edges with a sharp knife, and if you want to prettify your pie, decorate the top with the scraps cut into shapes of your choice.
- Glaze the top with beaten egg and then bake in the oven for about 45 minutes or until the pastry is golden brown. Allow the pie to stand for about 10 minutes before serving. Ideal vegetables to go with this pie are peas straight from the garden served with a knob of butter and a few sprigs of mint, and new potatoes cooked just enough for them retain a little bite.

Spicy Chicken Goujons

This recipe is my own alternative to chicken nuggets, which seem to be so popular with children today. These are very easy to make and you can always keep a batch in the freezer for when you have unexpected guests. If you are making them for adults, a few chilli flakes will give them an extra zing.

Serves 4

120 g (4 oz) natural yogurt
1 tbsp lemon juice
salt and freshly ground black pepper
2 large chicken breasts, cut into finger-sized strips
100 g (3½ oz) plain flour
1 large egg, beaten
200 g (7 oz) fresh breadcrumbs

Method

- Put the yogurt in a large bowl with the lemon juice and season with salt and pepper. Drop the chicken into the yogurt mixture and leave to soak for 2 hours; this will help to keep the chicken moist and tender.
- Preheat the oven to 200°C (400°F/Gas mark 6). Season the flour with salt and pepper. Place the flour in one bowl, the beaten egg in another, and the breadcrumbs in a third.
- Remove the chicken from the yogurt marinade, shaking off any excess. Dip each piece in the seasoned flour, then in the beaten egg, and finally coat with the breadcrumbs. Shake off any excess breadcrumbs and then lay the chicken pieces on a baking sheet, allowing space between each one. Drizzle with a little olive oil.
- Bake the chicken in the oven for about 15–20 minutes until golden brown, turning halfway through.

Curried Turkey

This basic curry paste will go with any meat, but was traditionally eaten in our house on Boxing Day with the leftover turkey. If you want to make a large batch of the paste it will keep in the fridge for up to 2 weeks or, alternatively, you can keep it in the freezer for up to 3 months. Make sure it is sealed in an airtight container, though, otherwise other items in your freezer may take on a spicy taste.

Makes 250–275 ml (8–9 fl oz)

2 tsp cumin seeds
2 tsp coriander seeds
1 tsp black peppercorns
3 tbsp groundnut oil
1 onion, peeled and finely chopped
4 cm (1½ in) fresh root ginger, finely chopped
4 garlic cloves, finely chopped
2 green chillies, deseeded and finely chopped
1 tsp turmeric
1 tsp smoked hot paprika
small bunch of fresh coriander
4 tbsp sieved tomatoes or passata

Method

- Start by roasting the cumin, coriander and black peppercorns in a hot, dry frying pan for about 3 minutes to release their full flavour. Put into a pestle and mortar and crush until you have a fine powder.
- Heat the oil in a frying pan and then add the chopped onion. Cook on a high heat until it is starting to go brown.
- Add the ginger, garlic and chilli and stir for about 30 seconds before turning the heat down to low. Cook for 15 minutes, stirring occasionally to prevent burning.

- Add the turmeric, paprika and fresh coriander and cook gently for a further 5 minutes. Again, stir occasionally – it is important not to burn it at this stage otherwise the final paste will taste bitter.
- Remove the pan from the heat and allow it to cool down a little. Put the contents of the pan into a blender together with 120 ml (4 fl oz) cold water. Whizz until you have a smooth paste.
- Put the paste into a saucepan and add the tomatoes or passata. Cook over a low heat for at least 30 minutes – the flavour will improve the longer you cook it.
- When you are ready to make your turkey curry, simply chop and fry another onion with some mushrooms. Add 2 tablespoons curry paste and enough water to make a smooth, creamy consistency. Add the leftover turkey and cook until it is warmed all the way through. You can vary the recipe if you like by adding some natural yogurt, crème fraîche or even coconut milk. Experiment until you get the heat and flavour you are happy with.

Quick Onion Bhajis

120 g (4 oz) plain flour
1 tsp garam masala
1 tsp turmeric
1 tsp salt
2 cloves garlic, finely chopped
1 bunch coriander, finely chopped
2 onions, peeled and sliced

Mix all the ingredients in a large bowl, with the exception of the onions, and gradually add water until you have a smooth coating batter. Add the onion and mix until it is thoroughly coated in the batter. Heat some oil in a large frying pan and drop tablespoon-sized balls of the onion mixture into the hot oil. Fry for a few minutes, turning once, until they are golden brown. Remove with a slotted spoon and drain on kitchen paper before serving.

Duck with Blackberry Sauce

This is a dish I serve for a special occasion, whether it is a birthday, anniversary or romantic meal for two. The wild blackberries complement the richness of the duck breast beautifully, so just wait until the fruit are bursting with flavour and go for a walk armed with a plastic bag or bowl to pick the berries. I always carry a walking stick with a curved end so that I can hook out-of-reach branches down to my height. Another tip – make sure you are wearing old clothes as they are bound to become stained!

Serves 2

50 g (2 oz) unsalted butter
4 shallots, finely chopped
1 garlic clove, finely chopped
2 sprigs of fresh thyme
1 tsp white sugar
100 ml (3½ fl oz) red wine
275 g (10 oz) wild blackberries
200 ml (7 fl oz) beef stock (see pages 12–13)
1 bay leaf
1 tsp cornflour
salt and freshly ground black pepper
2 free-range duck breasts

Method

- Melt the butter in a saucepan and add the shallots and garlic. Cook on a medium heat until they become translucent, but do not allow them to brown.
- Add the fresh thyme and sugar and cook until the sugar starts to caramelize. At this point add the red wine and cook until the liquid has reduced by three-quarters.
- Tip two-thirds of the blackberries into the saucepan and add the stock and bay leaf. Cook until the liquid has reduced by two-thirds.

- Pour the contents of the saucepan into a fine sieve and press with the back of a wooden spoon so that you push all the fruit purée into the sauce.
- Mix the cornflour with a little of the sauce until smooth and then add to the rest of the sauce in a clean saucepan. Cut the remaining blackberries in half and add them to the sauce. Return to the heat and cook gently, stirring constantly, until the sauce has thickened slightly. Set the sauce aside.
- Preheat the oven to 180°C (350°F/gas mark 4).
- Season the duck breasts on both sides and heat a dry ovenproof frying pan over a high heat. When the pan is really hot, gently put the duck breasts in the pan, skin side down, and fry for 2 minutes or until the skin has turned brown. Turn over and repeat on the other side. Put the frying pan into the oven and cook for a further 15 minutes.
- Allow the duck to stand for 5 minutes and then carve into thick slices. Arrange them neatly on a serving plate and pour the rich blackberry sauce over them.

Artichoke Mash with Spring Onions

To accompany the duck, why not try equal quantities of Jerusalem artichokes and potatoes mashed with a little butter and milk. Add some chopped spring onion just before serving.

The Perfect Roast Goose

Because goose is a dark, gamey meat that is full of fat, it is not the first choice for Christmas dinner these days. However, cooked properly on a rack so that all the fat drains off, it is a delicious alternative to chicken or turkey – and, of course, you have all that wonderful goose fat to roast your potatoes in. Before I put my goose in the oven I like to make a criss-cross pattern in the skin with a very sharp knife, making sure I do not cut into the flesh. I then place the bird onto a rack and pour boiling water over it. This not only helps to crisp the skin, but keeps the breast moist as well. I cook my stuffing in a separate tray as you do not need the cavity stuffed to keep the bird moist.

Serves 6

small bunch of sage, rosemary and thyme leaves
sea salt and whole black peppercorns
1 free-range goose, 5 kg (11 lb) in weight

For the gravy:
goose giblets
2 onions, roughly chopped
2 carrots, roughly chopped
sprig of fresh rosemary
sprig of fresh thyme
a few sage leaves
4 tbsp water
1 tbsp plain flour
60 ml (2 fl oz) red wine
1 tbsp demerara sugar

Method

- Preheat the oven to 220°C (425°F/Gas mark 7). Put the sage, rosemary and thyme into a pestle and mortar with the salt and black peppercorns and crush until you have a fine rubbing paste. Rub this paste all over the skin of the goose.

- ❖ Put the giblets, onions, carrots, herbs and water in a deep roasting pan . Put the goose on a wire rack over the top of them and cover it in kitchen foil. Place in the oven.
- ❖ After 45 minutes, reduce the heat to 180°C (350°F/Gas mark 4). The goose will take about 4½–5 hours to cook; allow 30 minutes per 450 g (1 lb) if you are cooking a larger or smaller bird. Because the goose will release a lot of fat, you will need to check that the roasting tray is not becoming too full at least once an hour. If need be, scoop some out carefully and set aside to roast your potatoes.
- ❖ For the last hour, remove the kitchen foil to allow the skin of the goose to go brown and crisp. At the end of the cooking time, test that the goose is done by inserting a skewer or the point of a knife into the meat where the legs join the body. Allow the juices to trickle down the skewer or knife and if they run clear the meat is ready.
- ❖ When you are satisfied that the meat is cooked, lift the goose carefully off the rack, place it on a board and allow to stand for at least 20 minutes before carving.
- ❖ Pour off the fat from the roasting tray, leaving the dark meat juices, vegetables, herbs and giblets to use for your gravy.
- ❖ Stir in the flour and, using a fork, gradually mash the vegetables. Add some water and allow the gravy to cook until it has thickened. Pour the gravy through a sieve into a pan, pressing the mushy vegetables through with the back of a wooden spoon. Put the gravy back onto the heat and add the red wine and the demerara sugar, which helps to remove some of the acidity from the wine. Bring back to the boil and cook until it has reduced by two-thirds.
- ❖ Carve your goose, pile it up onto a serving plate and serve with the gravy and plenty of Christmas vegetables.

See page 126 for the perfect stuffing to accompany the roast goose.

Stuffing to Accompany Goose

Of all the stuffings I have made to go with goose, this is by far my favourite and is also very apt for Christmas as it contains chestnuts and cranberries.

25 g (1 oz) unsalted butter
1 onion, finely chopped
2 celery sticks, finely chopped
2 garlic cloves, finely chopped
1 kg (2¼ lb) cooked chestnuts, chopped
150 g (5 oz) dried cranberries
1 tbsp fresh sage, chopped
1 tsp smoked sweet paprika
salt and freshly ground black pepper

Mix all the ingredients together, season well, then press into an oblong tin or make into stuffing balls. Bake in a preheated oven (200°C/400°F/Gas mark 6) for approximately 35 minutes, first drizzling with a little olive oil.

Braised Pheasant in Cider

If you live in the countryside, there is usually no shortage of pheasants during the shooting season. They have a rich, gamey meat, which works really well with the sweeter flavour of cider and apples. This recipe braises the meat, which means it stays very moist and tender and literally falls off the bone. If you are buying your pheasant from a butcher, ask him to cut it up into joints as this will make life a lot easier for you.

Serves 4

4 pheasant pieces on the bone
salt and freshly ground black pepper
2 tbsp olive oil
2 rashers of streaky bacon, cut into small strips
2 shallots, finely chopped
1 tbsp thyme leaves, removed from the stalk
550 ml (17 fl oz) cider
250 ml (8 fl oz) chicken stock (see pages 11–12)
150 ml (5 fl oz) single cream
25 g (1 oz) unsalted butter
2 dessert apples such as Braeburn, peeled and cut into eighths

Method

- Season the pheasant pieces with salt and pepper. Heat the olive oil in a large casserole dish and brown the pheasant on all sides. Remove from the dish and set aside.
- Fry the streaky bacon until crisp, using the same casserole dish. Add the chopped shallots and thyme and cook until the shallots become translucent. Put the pheasant back into the casserole dish and add the cider. Boil rapidly for about 2 minutes or until the quantity of liquid has reduced slightly.
- Add the stock and season with salt and pepper. Reduce the heat to a simmer, cover with a lid and cook gently for 1 hour.
- Remove the pheasant from the pan and turn up the heat again. Boil until the liquid has reduced by half. Whisk in the single cream and check the seasoning.
- Melt the butter in a frying pan and fry the apple pieces until they are browned on both sides. Be careful when turning them over as you do not want them to break up as they become softer.
- Add the apple to the sauce and pour over the pheasant pieces. Serve with new potatoes, mashed potatoes or celeriac mash with crisp cabbage.

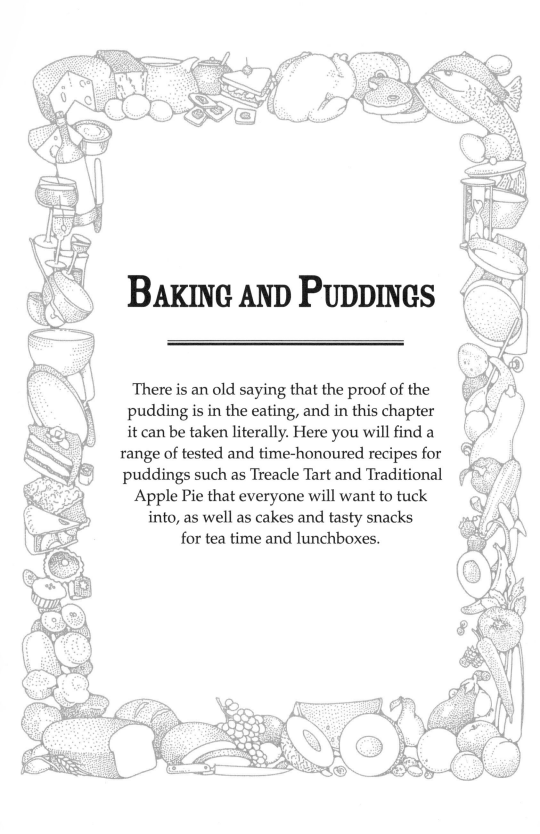

Baking and Puddings

There is an old saying that the proof of the pudding is in the eating, and in this chapter it can be taken literally. Here you will find a range of tested and time-honoured recipes for puddings such as Treacle Tart and Traditional Apple Pie that everyone will want to tuck into, as well as cakes and tasty snacks for tea time and lunchboxes.

Pastry and Pies

Many modern cooks do not make their own pastry because they believe it is too time-consuming or complicated, but this really is not the case: you just need to follow some simple guidelines. My grandmother told me that to make perfect pastry you need to have cold hands. I am not sure this is necessarily true, but working with the dough is certainly easier if your hands have first been chilled by holding them under the cold tap. The main tips for making light, mouth-watering pastry are to avoid over-handling the dough and to incorporate as much air as possible when rubbing the fat into the flour by lifting the ingredients as high as is practical while you work. Of course if you are very rushed there is still a good reason for buying readymade pastry, but if you do have the time to make your own it really is worth the effort and your guests will definitely taste the difference.

There are many types of pastry, but here I am including just two that will be all you need to make both sweet and savoury dishes: these are rough puff pastry (which is far simpler and quicker than ordinary puff pastry) and shortcrust.

Rough Puff Pastry

This recipe for puff pastry is very quick, yet the finished result is really light and flaky. It does not require endless folding and rolling like regular puff pastry and can be made the day before it is required as it benefits from resting in a cool place. The quantity given below is sufficient to cover a large pie, or to make 12 sausage rolls.

Makes about 300 g (10 oz)

225 g (8 oz) plain flour

½ tsp salt
185 g (6½ oz) chilled butter
90–120 ml (3–4 fl oz) cold water
1 tsp lemon juice

Method

- Start by sifting the flour and salt into a bowl as this helps to get air into the flour before you start.
- Cut the butter into small cubes and add to the flour. Mix, using a cold knife, to make sure that the butter pieces are totally covered with flour.
- Make a well in the centre and add the cold water and lemon juice. Mix the ingredients with a cold knife, only using your hands at the very last minute to form the mixture into a soft dough. The idea is to keep the dough as cold as possible while you work.
- Dust a pastry board or work surface and your rolling pin with some flour and then roll out the dough into a rectangle that is three times longer than it is wide.
- Fold the top third into the middle and the bottom third over the top and seal the edges by pinching them together with your finger and thumb.
- Roll out the dough again so that you form another rectangle as before. Fold the pastry and seal in the same way.
- Roll and fold the dough twice more in exactly the same way and then wrap it in clingfilm and place in the fridge for at least 30 minutes before you wish to use it.

Shortcrust Pastry

Just as in the recipe for rough puff pastry, try to keep all the ingredients and utensils as cold as possible. If you are making pastry on a really hot day, it is a good idea to chill the bowl first in the fridge to help keep everything cool. Although shortcrust pastry does not rise, you still need to incorporate air into the dough so that the finished product is nice and light. My grandmother always used lard alone, but I prefer a mixture of lard and butter and I have never had a failure yet.

Makes about 300 g (10 oz)

225 g (8 oz) plain flour
½ tsp salt
50 g (2 oz) chilled butter
50 g (2 oz) chilled lard
3–4 tbsp cold water

Method

- Start by sifting the flour and salt into a large bowl, lifting the sieve high to incorporate as much air as possible.
- Cut the butter and lard into small cubes and drop into the flour.
- Run your hands under cold water and dry thoroughly. Work the fat into the flour, using your fingertips, until the mixture resembles fine breadcrumbs.
- Make a well in the centre and gradually add the cold water, using a cold, round-bladed knife to start to bring the ingredients together. Once the dough begins to form a clump, use your hands to form it into a round ball.
- Wrap the dough in clingfilm and place in the fridge for at least 30 minutes.
- Take the dough from the fridge about 10 minutes before you are ready to use it. Remove the clingfilm and gently knead the dough on a floured surface. Finish by rolling it out to the desired thickness and size.

Traditional Apple Pie

Apple pie, full of delightfully juicy fruit, will always be one of my favourite desserts. I prefer to use Bramleys because they contain less sugar than dessert varieties, they retain their lovely tangy flavour once cooked and they always have a soft texture to complement the crumbly pastry.

Serves 6

300 g (10 oz) shortcrust pastry (see pages 131–132)
1 tbsp plain flour
175 g (6 oz) sugar
½ tsp ground nutmeg
½ tsp ground cinnamon
1 tsp salt
4 large Bramley apples, peeled, cored and sliced
50 g (2 oz) unsalted butter
1 tsp lemon juice

Method

- Preheat the oven to 220°C (425°F/Gas mark 7).
- Divide your pastry dough in half and roll out 2 sheets slightly larger than a pie dish measuring 25 cm (10 in) in diameter.
- Line the pie dish with one of the sheets and trim off any excess pastry. Place in the fridge until you are ready to put in the filling.
- Mix together the flour, sugar, nutmeg, cinnamon and salt in a large bowl and then stir in the apple pieces until they are coated in the mixture.
- Remove the pie dish from the fridge and pour the apple mixture on top of the pastry base. Dot with small pieces of butter and sprinkle with a little lemon juice.
- Take the second sheet of pastry and roll it around your rolling pin. Gently unroll it over the top of the pie dish and then seal the edges using a fork. Cut slits in the top to allow the steam to escape and trim off excess pastry.
- Bake in the oven for 40–45 minutes, or until the pastry is golden brown and you can see the apple juices bubbling through the slits in the top of the pie.
- Allow the pie to stand for 10 minutes before slicing into portions. Serve with some clotted cream, ice cream or home-made custard (see page 134).

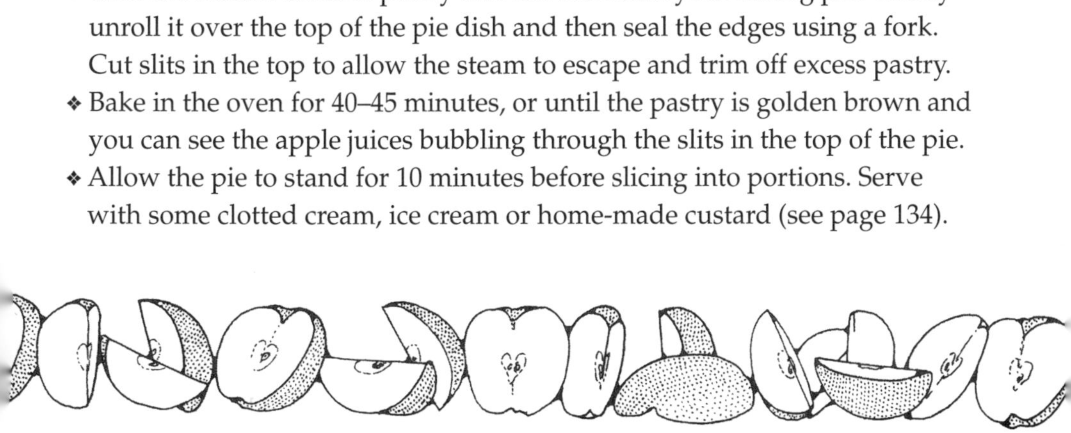

Grandmother's Creamy Custard

1 vanilla pod
150 ml (5 fl oz) milk
150 ml (5 fl oz) double cream
3 egg yolks
1 tsp cornflour
25 g (1 oz) caster sugar

- Split the vanilla pod lengthways and then scoop out the seeds inside with a teaspoon.
- Pour the milk and the cream into a saucepan and add the vanilla seeds and pod.
- Over moderate heat, bring the milk and cream mixture just to simmering point, but do not allow it to boil.
- Whisk together the egg yolks, cornflour and sugar until light and frothy.
- Remove the vanilla pod from the milk in the saucepan and then, whisking vigorously, gradually pour the milk into the egg mixture.
- When you have used up all the milk, pour everything back into the saucepan and put it back onto a gentle heat. Stir continuously until the custard has thickened.
- Pour the custard into a serving jug and cover it with some clingfilm to prevent a skin from forming over the top.

If you would like to make a chocolate custard, break up 100 g (3½ oz) dark chocolate and add it when you put the custard back on the heat. The leftover egg whites could be used to make some meringues (see pages 70–71).

Cheese Straws

It can be hard to think of something different but homemade to put in a child's lunchbox. My mother would sometimes make a batch of cheese straws and they made a lovely change from sandwiches. This recipe comes from my grandmother's handwritten cookbook and I think that the old recipes that have been handed down through the family are by far the best.

The number will depend on how large you make your straws!

75 g (3 oz) plain flour
salt and freshly ground black pepper
1 tsp paprika
½ tsp bicarbonate of soda
50 g (2 oz) chilled unsalted butter
1 egg yolk, beaten
75 g (3 oz) mature Cheddar cheese, grated

Method

- Preheat the oven to 200°C (400°F/Gas mark 6).
- Sieve the flour, salt and pepper, paprika and bicarbonate of soda into a large bowl.
- Cut the butter into small cubes and drop it into the flour mixture. Now rub the butter into the flour as you did for the shortcrust pastry on pages 131–132, using cool fingertips. Once it resembles fine breadcrumbs add the beaten egg yolk and knead with your hands until a soft dough is formed.
- Flour a pastry board or work surface and your rolling pin and then roll out the dough until it is about 1 cm (½ in) thick. Now, using a sharp knife, cut the dough into strips about 1 cm (½ in) wide to any length you like.
- Bake in the oven for 10–15 minutes or until the cheese straws are golden brown.
- If you wish to add some other flavours, brush the cheese straws in milk and then roll them in some sesame seeds, poppy seeds or any other type of seeds you fancy.

MINCE PIES

I do not know anyone who does not love a warm mince pie with a big dollop of cream on the top. Although traditionally eaten at Christmas, mince pies make a lovely treat at any time of the year. Once you have all the ingredients, making your own mincemeat is simple – it is just a matter of putting everything in a big bowl and mixing it all together with a wooden spoon.

Makes 4 jars

350 g (12 oz) sultanas
350 g (12 oz) raisins
350 g (12 oz) currants
175 g (6 oz) flaked almonds
3 large Bramley apples, grated
400 g (14 oz) dark brown sugar
grated zest and juice of 2 lemons
grated zest and juice of 1 orange
1 tsp ground nutmeg
½ tsp ground cloves
½ tsp ground cinnamon
½ tsp ground ginger
175 g (6 oz) vegetable suet
120 ml (4 fl oz) brandy

Method

- Place all the above ingredients in a large bowl and mix thoroughly with a wooden spoon.
- Sterilize your glass jars by putting them in the oven at 170°C (325°F/ Gas mark 3) for 10 minutes or, if you have a dishwasher, simply put them through the cycle and take them out while they are still hot.
- Put the mincemeat in the jars while they are hot, put a circle of greaseproof paper over the top and then seal with a lid.
- To make the mince pies, make a batch of shortcrust pastry (see pages

131–132), roll it out until it is about 1 cm (½ in) thick and then, using a biscuit cutter, cut out twelve 7.5 cm (3 in) circles for the bases and twelve 6 cm (2½ in) circles for the lids.

- Preheat the oven to 200°C (400°F/Gas mark 6). Grease some patty tins lightly and then line them with the larger circles. Fill each with mincemeat until it is level with the edges of the pastry.
- Wet the edges of the smaller circles with a little water and then press them down on top of the mincemeat, making sure you seal the edges with your fingers.
- Make a little slit in the top of each one and sprinkle generously with caster sugar. Bake near the top of the oven for about 20–25 minutes or until they are golden brown.
- Allow to cool on a wire tray and then store in an airtight container for up to 5 days – if they last that long!

Treacle Tart

Treacle tart is a wonderful way of using up day-old bread. In spite of its name, it is actually made with treacle's lighter-coloured cousin, golden syrup.

Serves 6

300 g (10 oz) shortcrust pastry (see pages 131–132)
225 g (8 oz) white bread
120 ml (4 fl oz) golden syrup
pinch of salt
zest of ½ lemon
½ tsp ground ginger

Method

- Preheat the oven to 200°C (400°F/Gas mark 7). Make a batch of shortcrust pastry dough and use it to line a flan tin. Bake it 'blind' by pricking the base, placing a layer of greaseproof paper over the top of the uncooked pastry and then weighting it down with some dried beans. Bake for 6–10 minutes. Remove the lining and allow the pastry case to cool down a little before adding the filling.

- Reduce the oven heat to 190°C (375°C/Gas mark 5). Make breadcrumbs by putting the bread in a food processor and whizzing until you have crumbs of a fine consistency. (Breadcrumbs can be made in advance and kept in the freezer for use whenever you need them).
- Put the breadcrumbs in a jug or bowl and then warm the golden syrup in a saucepan over a gentle heat. Pour the syrup over the breadcrumbs then add the salt, lemon zest and ginger and mix thoroughly.
- Pour the filling into the pastry case and bake in the oven for 20–25 minutes. The pastry should be a lovely golden brown and the filling should have set a little. A word of caution: do not serve this dessert straight from the oven as the syrup filling will be very hot indeed.

Strawberry Teatime Treats

Make a batch of shortcrust pastry (see pages 131–132), line some patty tins, prick the base with a fork and then bake for 15 minutes in a preheated oven at 200°C (400°F/Gas mark 6). Leave to cool while you make the filling.

100 ml/3½ fl oz) whipping cream
2 tbsp caster sugar
1 tbsp fresh orange juice
225 g (8 oz) freshly picked strawberries, hulled

- Whisk the cream until it is thick and then gradually whisk in the sugar and orange juice.
- Set aside 6 whole strawberries for decoration and mash the rest. Fold the mashed strawberries into the cream.
- Just before you are ready to serve, spoon the filling into the pastry cases and top each tart with slices of fresh strawberry.

Simple Cakes and Biscuits

Teatime would not be right if there were not a choice of cakes and biscuits to have with a hot cup of tea. They do not need to be fancy pastries that you would see in the window of a patisserie; simple, old-fashioned recipes that always adorned Grandmother's table are just as popular with all ages.

Victoria Sponge Cake

This sponge cake was named after Queen Victoria, who always liked a slice of cake with her afternoon tea. It is very easy to make and was traditionally served with a layer of fresh cream and jam in the centre rather than being iced. The quantities are really easy to remember as you need the same amount of fat, sugar and flour.

Makes an 18 cm (7in) cake

115 g (4 oz) unsalted butter, at room temperature
115 g (4 oz) caster sugar
2 eggs, at room temperature
115 g (4 oz) self-raising flour
pinch of salt
300 ml (10 fl oz) double cream
5–6 tbsp jam such as strawberry
1 tbsp icing sugar

Method

- Preheat the oven to 180°C (350°F/Gas mark 4). Grease and lightly flour the bottom of 2 round cake tins, about 18 cm (7 in) in diameter.
- Put the butter and sugar in a large bowl and cream together until the

mixture is pale and creamy in texture. You can do this by hand, but it is quicker if you use an electric whisk.

- Break an egg into the bowl together with a spoonful of the flour – this will stop the mixture from curdling. Whisk for 2 minutes and then add the second egg and beat for a further couple of minutes.
- You need to avoid losing the air that you have incorporated into the mixture by beating it so, using a metal spoon, gently fold the remaining flour and a pinch of salt into the cake mixture until it is thoroughly mixed.
- Divide the cake mixture evenly between the two cake tins and bake in the oven for 20 minutes. On no account be tempted to open the door to check it before this time, otherwise you risk a heavy, deflated cake as the cooler air hits it.
- At the end of the cooking time, the cake should be golden brown in colour and firm to the touch. You can test to see if it is ready by inserting a knife into the centre of the cake – if it comes out clean then you can remove the cake from the oven.
- Turn the cake out onto a wire rack to cool. Once it is completely cold, whisk the double cream and spread it on one half of the cake. Spread with strawberry jam (or any flavour you like) and then sandwich the two halves together. Sprinkle the top with sifted icing sugar and give your cake pride of place at the centre of the tea table.

Fruit Cake

A fruit cake can always take pride of place on a tea table and in this recipe the addition of some dates makes it just that little bit more special.

Makes an 18 cm (7in) cake

140 g (5 oz) butter, softened
175 g (6 oz) Demerara sugar
240 g (8½ oz) self-raising flour
¼ tsp salt

1 tsp ground cinnamon
2 eggs
100 g (3½ oz) raisins
100 g (3½ oz) sultanas
100 g (3½ oz) dates, chopped
grated zest of 1 orange
grated zest of 1 lemon
75 ml (2½ fl oz) milk
2 tbsp apricot jam

Method

- Preheat the oven to 180°C (350°F/Gas mark 4). Grease and lightly flour a deep cake tin about 18 cm (7 in) in diameter.
- Cream together the butter and sugar until the mixture is light and fluffy in appearance.
- Sift the flour, salt and cinnamon into another bowl.
- Add the eggs to the butter/sugar mixture one at a time with a little of the flour, beating well after each addition.
- Add the flour, raisins, sultanas, dates, orange and lemon zest and milk. Mix well until all the ingredients are thoroughly combined.
- Turn the mixture into your prepared cake tin and bake for about 1½ hours in the centre of the preheated oven. The top of the cake should be golden brown when it has finished cooking, but test by inserting a skewer into the centre of the cake; if it comes out clean the cake is ready.
- Allow the cake to cool for 5 minutes in the tin and then turn out onto a wire rack to cool completely.
- Put the apricot jam in a small pan and heat over a medium heat until it becomes runny. Brush the top of the cake with the jam and allow to cool before serving.

GOOEY CHOCOLATE BROWNIES

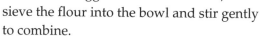

This recipe was sent to me by my sister, who lives in the USA, and I have never found a better one for chocolate brownies – the middle stays really gooey. These brownies hit the spot when you have a craving for chocolate.

Makes 20 brownies

375 g (13 oz) unsalted butter
375 g (13 oz) good-quality dark chocolate
6 eggs
450 g (1 lb) caster sugar
½ tsp salt
1 tsp vanilla essence
225 g (8 oz) plain flour

Method

- Preheat the oven to 180°C (350°F/Gas mark 4). Line a baking tray with greaseproof paper which has been greased with butter.
- Break up the chocolate and place it, along with the butter, in a heatproof bowl over a pan of simmering water until the chocolate has melted, stirring occasionally. Do not allow the bowl to come in contact with the water.
- Break the eggs into a large bowl, add the sugar, salt and vanilla essence and whisk until light and frothy.
- Add the melted chocolate and butter to the egg mixture in the bowl, then sieve the flour into the bowl and stir gently to combine.
- Pour the mixture onto the lined baking tray, making sure that it is spread out evenly. Bake in the oven for 20–25 minutes until the top has started to set but the middle is still gooey.
- Allow the mixture to cool in the tin and then cut into slices.

Shortbread

Shortbread is a rich, buttery biscuit that quite simply melts in the mouth. Eat it as a treat on its own, or with strawberries and cream for a special treat.

Makes 12 biscuits

225 g (8 oz) unsalted butter, at room temperature
110 g (4 oz) caster sugar
pinch of salt
225 g (8 oz) plain flour
100 g (3½ oz) cornflour

Method

- Preheat the oven to 160°C (325°F/Gas mark 3).
- Cream together the butter, sugar and salt in a large bowl, using a hand whisk, until light, fluffy and pale in colour.
- Sieve the flour and cornflour into the mixture, holding the sieve as high as possible to incorporate air. Mix gently together until the ingredients are thoroughly combined, but do not overwork at this stage.
- Lightly flour a board or work surface and then knead the dough gently – the less you handle the shortbread dough the crumblier it will be when cooked. Flour your rolling pin and then roll out the shortbread between 2 sheets of greaseproof paper until it is 1 cm (½ in) thick. Use biscuit cutters to cut out different shapes, or alternatively roll the dough into a circular shape and score it into sections so that it can divided after it is cooked. Prick the surface of the shortbread dough with a fork and then place it on a lightly greased baking tray.
- Bake in the oven for 20–25 minutes or until the shortbread is a pale golden brown.
- Sprinkle the shortbread with a little extra caster sugar and then leave to cool on a wire rack. If you have cooked it in one piece, cut down through the score marks while the shortbread is still warm.
- Store the shortbread in an airtight container.

Oaty Flapjacks

There is nothing fancy about these flapjacks – they just have the traditional ingredients, to be eaten as a snack at any time of day. You can add fruit, nuts or chocolate chips if you want to make them more elaborate, but I like them just as they are.

Makes 12–20 flapjacks

200 g (7 oz) porridge oats
25 g (1 oz) plain flour
pinch of salt
100 g (3½ oz) unsalted butter
75 g (3 oz) demerara sugar
2 tbsp golden syrup

Method

- Preheat the oven to 180°C (350°F/Gas mark 4). Grease and lightly flour a baking tray that is at least 2.5 cm (½ in) deep.
- In a large bowl, mix together the oats, flour and salt.
- Melt the butter, sugar and golden syrup in a saucepan over gentle heat until the sugar has completely dissolved. Stir occasionally to make sure that the mixture is not sticking to the bottom of the pan. Pour into the oat mixture and stir thoroughly to combine.
- Pour the oaty mixture onto the baking tray and spread it out using the back of a spoon. Bake in the oven for 20 minutes or until it is golden brown and fairly firm to the touch.
- Remove from the oven and while it is still hot, mark it out into squares or rectangles. Allow to cool in the baking tray, then cut into the shapes you have chosen and store in an airtight container.

Baking Bread

You might feel that making bread is just too much hard work, but let me assure you it really is worth the effort. Nothing compares to the smell and taste of a lovely crusty loaf that has just come out of the oven. Because it does not contain any preservatives homemade bread will not stay as fresh as supermarket loaves, but if you slice it up as soon as it is cold and place it in the freezer it will be fresh when defrosted.

Basic White Loaf

Makes 1 large loaf or 2 small

600 g (1 lb 5 oz) strong white bread flour
1 tsp salt
1 tsp dried bread yeast
1 tsp caster sugar
450 ml (15 fl oz) warm water
butter for greasing

Method

- Sieve the flour into a large bowl and then add the salt, yeast and sugar.
- Make a well in the centre of the flour, then gradually add the water. Using your hands, work the flour into the liquid until you have a soft dough ball in the centre of your bowl, leaving the sides totally clean.
- Place the dough onto a floured board and knead until it starts to become springy in your hands.
- Cover the dough with a clean, damp tea towel and then leave to prove at room temperature until it has doubled in size – this can take up to 2 hours.

- Grease your loaf tin with butter and then sprinkle with flour. For 1 large loaf you will need a 900 g (2 lb) tin; for 2 smaller ones you will need 450 g (1 lb) tins.
- When the dough has doubled in size, sprinkle your board with a little more flour and then knead for another 2–3 minutes.
- Put the dough into your loaf tin(s) and leave to prove again at room temperature for another hour. You will find that the dough has risen considerably and is starting to go over the side of the tin.
- Preheat the oven to 230°C (450°F/Gas mark 8). Bake the loaf for 35–40 minutes for 1 large loaf, or 30–35 minutes for 2 smaller ones. To check whether the loaf is cooked, simply tap the bottom with your knuckles – if it is ready it should make a hollow sound.
- Leave to cool on a wire rack before slicing.

Basic Wholemeal Loaf

Makes 1 large loaf or 2 small

500 g (1 lb 2 oz) wholewheat bread flour
2 tsp salt
2 tsp dried bread yeast
1 tsp light brown sugar
400 ml (14 fl oz) warm water

Method

- Follow the instructions for the basic white loaf above to make this healthier version of your daily loaf.

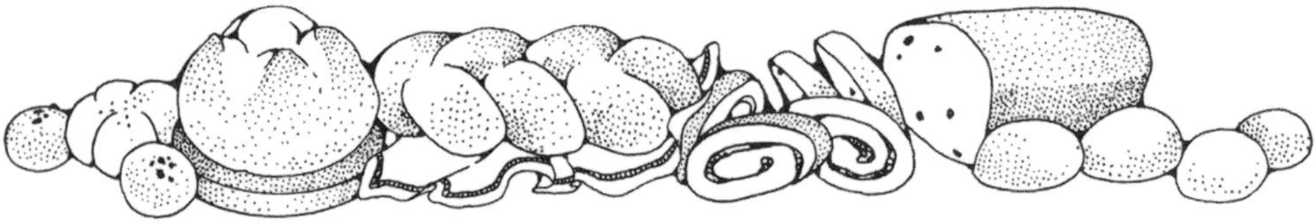

Soda Bread

If you do not have time to wait for a loaf to prove, have a go at this traditional soda bread. It does not require kneading and can be ready within an hour if you have unexpected guests.

Makes 1 large loaf

400 g (14 oz) plain white flour
1 tsp bicarbonate of soda
1 tsp salt
1 tsp caster sugar
350 ml (12 fl oz) buttermilk

Method

- Preheat the oven to 230°C (450°F/Gas mark 8).
- Sieve the flour, bicarbonate of soda and salt into a large bowl. Add the sugar and then make a well in the centre.
- Pour in most of the buttermilk, leaving a little in the bottom of the jug, and then start to work the flour into the liquid using your fingers. You should avoid kneading the dough as this can make it too heavy – your aim is just to mix the ingredients until you have a soft, pliable dough.
- When the dough comes away cleanly from the side of the bowl, turn it out onto a floured board and bring the edges into the middle a few times, pushing it down with your knuckles.
- Gently pat the dough into a circle approximately 4 cm (1½ in) thick. Using a sharp knife, cut a cross in the top and place the dough on a greased and floured baking tray.
- Bake in the oven for 15 minutes, then turn the heat down to 200°C (400°F/Gas mark 6) for a further 30 minutes. When it is cooked the loaf should be golden brown and sound hollow when tapped on the bottom.
- Leave to cool on a wire rack before slicing.

Fruity Tea Bread

My recipe for tea bread could be described as a mixture between a fruit cake and a fruit loaf. It is delicious sliced, buttered and served with an afternoon cup of tea.

Makes 1 × 450 g (1 lb) loaf

175 g (6 oz) light brown sugar
150 ml (5 fl oz) hot, freshly-made tea
225 g (8 oz) sultanas
115 g (4 oz) raisins
115 g (4 oz) currants
1 egg, beaten
225 g (8 oz) self raising flour
½ tsp cinnamon

Method

- Start by adding the sugar to the tea. Stir well until the sugar has dissolved.
- Add all the fruit to the tea and mix well. Cover the bowl with clingfilm and then leave overnight to give the fruit time to swell.
- The following day, add the beaten egg to the fruit mixture and mix thoroughly. Sieve the flour and cinnamon into the fruit mixture and again mix well.
- Preheat the oven to 160°C (325°F/Gas mark 3). Grease and lightly flour a 450 g (1 lb) loaf tin.
- Put your tea bread mixture into the loaf tin and bake in the oven for 1–1½ hours. To test that your loaf is ready, insert a knife or a skewer into the centre – if it comes out clean the loaf is cooked.
- Turn out on a wire rack and leave to cool before slicing.

Scones

I could not write a recipe book without including my two favourite scones recipes, both of which I guarantee you will make time and time again.

Classic Scones

Makes 12 scones

250 g (9 oz) plain flour
4 tsp baking powder
½ tsp salt
1 tbsp caster sugar
50 g (2 oz) unsalted butter, cut into small cubes
2 eggs, beaten
175 ml (6 fl oz) double cream

Method

- Preheat the oven to 220°C (425°F/Gas mark 7). Grease and lightly flour a baking tray.
- Sieve the flour, baking powder and salt into a large bowl. Add the sugar and then the butter. Work the mixture with your fingertips until it resembles coarse breadcrumbs.
- Mix the beaten eggs and cream together, then add this to the dry ingredients, trying not to stir the mixture too much. Once it is mixed and you have a soft dough, turn it out onto a floured board and roll it out until it is about 1 cm (½ in) thick.
- Cut into circles using a biscuit cutter and place on the greased baking tray.
- Bake in the oven for 15–18 minutes or until the scones are starting to turn golden brown. Leave on a wire rack to cool and serve with clotted cream and jam.

Drop Scones

Drop scones can be eaten as either a savoury or a sweet snack. My grandson loves them with a fried egg on top, accompanied by a couple of rashers of crispy bacon.

Makes 12 scones

115 g (4 oz) self raising flour
a pinch of salt
50 g (2 oz) caster sugar
1 egg, beaten
about 4 tbsp milk

Method

- Put the flour, salt and sugar in a large bowl. Add the beaten egg and then gradually whisk in the milk a little at a time until you have a thick batter.
- Allow the batter to stand for 10 minutes while you heat up a well-greased griddle or heavy-based frying pan. Drop spoonfuls of the batter onto the hot griddle, allowing plenty of space between them. Cook until the underside is golden brown and bubbles are starting to appear on the surface. Turn over and cook the other side. That is all there is to it!

Puddings

Why is it that even after a large meal you always have a bit of space for a pudding? I still think that many of the traditional puddings are best, and it is hard to beat a creamy rice pudding with a lovely brown skin peppered with fresh nutmeg. Fruit pies and crumbles served with custard or cream are always popular in my household and I try to stick to fruits that are in season.

Rice Pudding

The traditional way to serve rice pudding is with a generous blob of colourful jam in the centre of the bowl. It may not be a sophisticated approach, but it adds to the heartwarming effect of this dish.

Serves 6

200 g (7 oz) pudding rice
115 g (4 oz) granulated sugar
300 ml (10 fl oz) double cream
200 ml (7 fl oz) milk
1 vanilla pod, split, seeds removed
1 tsp freshly grated nutmeg

Method

- Preheat the oven to 160°C (325°F/gas mark 3).
- Place the rice and sugar in a large ovenproof pudding dish and stir to combine. Mix together the cream and milk and add the vanilla seeds. Pour this over the top of the rice and then sprinkle generously with the nutmeg.
- Cover the dish with kitchen foil and cook in the oven for 1½ hours. Remove the foil and cook for another 20 minutes or until the top has formed a brown skin. Serve with a dollop of jam of your choice.

Tapioca Pudding

This creamy classic with the subtle hint of vanilla was one of my favourite puddings when I was growing up.

Serves 4

75 g (3 oz) tapioca
700 ml (1 pint 3 fl oz) milk
150 ml (5 fl oz) double cream
4 tbsp caster sugar
1 vanilla pod, split and seeds removed

Method

- Put all the ingredients into a large saucepan. Bring to the boil, stirring continuously, then turn down the heat and simmer for 30–35 minutes, stirring from time to time, until the tapioca has become thick and creamy. Serve in individual bowls with fruit sauce (see opposite).

Semolina Pudding

Semolina pudding is a dish that people either love or hate; to some it is an unwanted reminder of school dinners. However, cooked properly it is a delicious sweet and creamy dish.

Serves 4

25 g (1 oz) unsalted butter
700 ml (1 pint 3 fl oz) milk
115 g (4 oz) semolina
115 g (4 oz) sugar
1 tsp ground cinnamon
2 egg yolks

Method

- Preheat the oven to 180°C (350°F/Gas mark 4). Butter a glass pudding dish.
- Pour the milk into a saucepan and heat until it is just about to boil. Remove from the heat and gradually add the semolina, whisking vigorously to avoid lumpiness. Return to the heat and gradually bring to the boil, whisking continuously, until the semolina is thickened and smooth.
- Take the pan off the heat again and stir in the sugar, cinnamon and egg yolks. Mix to combine the ingredients.
- Pour the semolina into the greased pudding dish, sprinkle the top with a little more cinnamon and then bake in the oven for 35–40 minutes.
- Serve in individual bowls with a little jam or fruit sauce (see below).

Grandmother's Fruit Sauce

This fruity sauce can liven up any dessert whether it is pancakes, waffles, ice cream or rice or tapioca pudding.

450 g (1 lb) mixed fruit – strawberries, raspberries, blackberries
1 tbsp cornflour
2 tbsp lemon juice
sugar to sweeten

- Place the fruit in a large saucepan and cook with a little water. Do not sweeten at this stage – you can adjust the sweetness at the end.
- Allow the fruit to cool and then put it into a blender and blend until it is smooth. Return it to the saucepan. Mix the cornflour with a little water to make a smooth paste, add to the fruit with the lemon juice and cook over a gentle heat until it thickens. Add sugar a little at a time until you reach the required sweetness.

Jam Roly Poly

This jam roly poly is easy to make and very comforting when served with a dollop of custard on a chilly winter's evening.

Serves 4–6

250 g (9 oz) self raising flour
½ tsp salt
125 g (4½ oz) vegetarian suet
4 tbsp raspberry or strawberry jam, warmed
1 tbsp milk
1 egg, beaten
caster sugar for dusting

Method

- Preheat the oven to 200°C (400°F/Gas mark 6).
- Sift the flour and salt into a large bowl. Add the suet and enough cold water to form a soft dough, using your hands. Add the water slowly – the dough must not become too sticky to roll out.
- Turn the dough out onto a floured board and then roll it out into a rectangle of approximately 20 x 30 cm (8 x 12 in).
- Warm the jam in a small saucepan and then spread it gently over the top of the dough rectangle.
- Brush the edges with milk then gradually roll the rectangle towards you and seal the final fold by pressing down gently with the end of a fork.
- Brush the outside of the roly poly with beaten egg and then roll it in some caster sugar to finish.
- Bake in the oven for 35–40 minutes or until it is a light golden colour. Slice and serve with a portion of hot custard (see page 134).

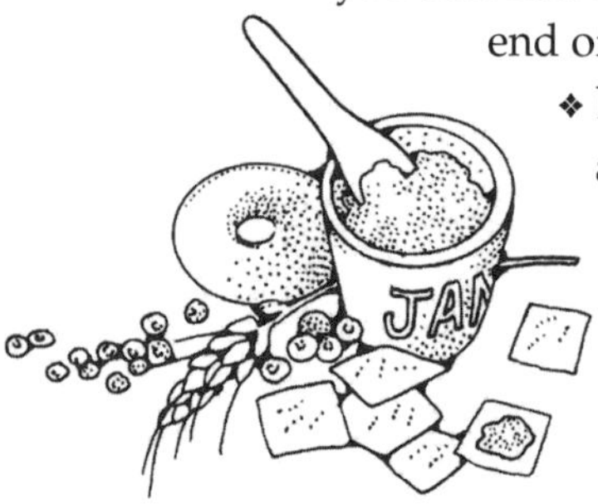

Eve's Pudding

As the apples stew in the bottom of the pie dish, the sponge on the top soaks up their juices and absorbs all the flavours of the fruit. I prefer to use eating apples rather than cooking apples when making Eve's pudding as it means you can cut down on the amount of sugar used.

Serves 4

4 eating apples such as Braeburn, peeled, cored and sliced
50 g (2 oz) self-raising flour
¼ tsp salt
½ tsp baking powder
30 g (1½ oz) unsalted butter
50 g (2 oz) caster sugar
1 egg

Method

- Preheat the oven to 180°C (350°F/Gas mark 4). Grease a large ovenproof baking dish with butter.
- Cook the apples in a large saucepan over gentle heat for about 5–10 minutes until they become soft, then transfer them to the dish.
- Sieve the flour, salt and baking powder into a bowl.
- In a separate bowl, cream together the butter and sugar until pale and creamy. Add the egg and whisk for 2 minutes.
- Using a metal spoon, fold the flour into the butter mixture, trying to work in as much air as possible as you go.
- Spread the cake mixture evenly over the top of the apples in the baking dish.
- Bake in the oven for 10–15 minutes or until the sponge topping has risen and is springy when you press it with your finger. Serve with ice cream, whipped cream or custard (see page 134).

Rhubarb and Strawberry Crumble

This is a combination that I discovered only a couple of years ago, but it has been a very popular pairing of flavours and one that I highly recommend. Of course crumble topping can be used with any type of fruit, so experiment with different combinations to see if they work.

Serves 4

25 g (1 oz) butter
625 g (1 lb 6 oz) rhubarb, cut into even-sized chunks
250 g (9 oz) strawberries, hulled
50 g (2 oz) caster sugar
grated zest of 1 orange

For the crumble:
115 g (4 oz) plain flour
115 g (4 oz) caster sugar
125 g (4½ oz) butter, cut into small cubes
75 g (2½ oz) porridge oats

Method

- Preheat the oven to 200°C (400°F/Gas mark 6). Grease an ovenproof dish with the butter.
- Place the rhubarb in the greased ovenproof dish and lay the strawberries on top. Sprinkle with the caster sugar and the grated zest of 1 orange.
- To make the crumble, mix the flour and sugar. Add the butter and, using your fingers, work the butter and flour until the mixture resembles coarse breadcrumbs. Add the porridge oats and then sprinkle the crumble over the top of the fruit. Bake in the oven for 30 minutes or until the top is golden brown.

Blueberry Jelly

You can use any fruit you like to make jelly, so although blueberries are given here, do experiment with different flavours. Rose-hip jelly is a classic autumn favourite, for example, using rose hips from the garden or hedgerows.

Serves 4–6

4 sheets of gelatine
225 g (8 oz) blueberries
300 ml (10 fl oz) blueberry juice (100% concentrate)

Method

- Soak the gelatine in water for 5 minutes until it becomes soft.
- Put the blueberries in a saucepan with the blueberry juice. Bring to the boil and then lower the heat until the mixture is simmering gently. Cook for 5–10 minutes or until the blueberries are soft.
- Press the mixture through a fine sieve to form a purée. Do not be tempted to put the mixture into a blender as you do not want the skins in the jelly.
- Shake the gelatine to remove any excess water. Add to the hot purée and stir until it has dissolved completely.
- Divide the jelly into tumblers and place in the fridge overnight to set.

Gooseberry Fool

The fruit fool, or 'foole', was first mentioned as a dessert in 1598, and has remained popular ever since for its very light and fruity flavour.

Serves 6

450 g (1 lb) gooseberries, topped and tailed
4 tbsp caster sugar
300 ml (10 fl oz) double cream

Method

- Put the gooseberries in a saucepan with the sugar. Bring to the boil and then reduce the heat to a simmer. Cook for about 10 minutes or until the gooseberries are starting to burst and are soft. Allow them to cool and then crush them using a fork. Whip the cream until it stands in peaks and then fold it into the fruit purée. Chill before serving.

Index